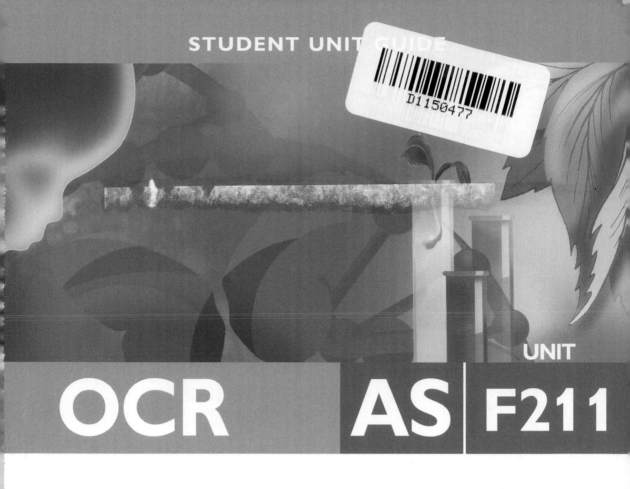

UNIT

OCR AS | F211

Biology

Cells, Exchange and Transport

Richard Fosbery

Philip Allan Updates, an imprint of Hodder Education, part of Hachette UK, Market Place, Deddington, Oxfordshire OX15 0SE

Orders

Bookpoint Ltd, 130 Milton Park, Abingdon, Oxfordshire OX14 4SB
tel: 01235 827720
fax: 01235 400454
e-mail: uk.orders@bookpoint.co.uk
Lines are open 9.00 a.m.–5.00 p.m., Monday to Saturday, with a 24-hour message answering service. You can also order through the Philip Allan Updates website: www.philipallan.co.uk

© Philip Allan Updates 2008

ISBN 978-0-340-95811-7

First printed 2008
Impression number 5 4 3 2
Year 2013 2012 2011 2010 2009

This guide has been written specifically to support students preparing for the OCR AS Biology Unit F211 examination. The content has been neither approved nor endorsed by OCR and remains the sole responsibility of the author.

Typeset by Fakenham Photosetting Ltd, Fakenham, Norfolk
Printed by MPG Books, Bodmin

Hachette UK's policy is to use papers that are natural, renewable and recyclable products and made from wood grown in sustainable forests. The logging and manufacturing processes are expected to conform to the environmental regulations of the country of origin.

Contents

Introduction

■ ■ ■

Content Guidance

■ ■ ■

Questions and Answers

Introduction

About this guide

This guide is the first of two that cover the OCR AS Specification in biology. It is intended to help you prepare for **Unit F211: Cells, Exchange and Transport**. It is divided into three sections:

- **Introduction** — this gives advice on how to use the guide to help your learning and revision and on how to prepare for the examination.
- **Content Guidance** — here you will find key facts, key concepts and links with other parts of the AS/A2 Biology course; you should find the **Focus on practical skills** sections useful for the practical work which is assessed in Unit F213. The **links** should help to show you how information in this unit is useful preparation for other units.
- **Questions and Answers** — here there are questions on each of the six sections in Unit F211, together with answers written by two candidates and examiner's comments.

This is not just a revision aid. This is a guide to the whole unit and you can use it throughout the 2 years of your course if you decide to go on to A2.

The **Content Guidance** section will help you to:

- organise your notes and check that you have highlighted the important points (key facts) — little 'chunks' of knowledge that you can remember
- check that you understand the links to practical work, since you will need your knowledge of this unit when doing the practical tasks in Unit F213: Practical Skills in Biology 1
- understand how these little 'chunks' fit into the wider picture; this will help:
  - to support Units F212 and F213 (you need knowledge of this unit for the other two units in AS)
  - to support the A2 units, if you decide to continue the course

The **Questions and Answers** section will help you to:

- check the way examiners ask questions at AS
- understand what examiners mean by terms like 'explain' and 'describe'
- interpret the question material, especially any data that the examiners give you
- write concisely and answer the questions that the examiners set

AS biology

The diagram below shows you the three units that make up the AS course. You should have a copy of the specification for the whole course. Keep it in your file with your notes and refer to it constantly. You should know exactly which topics you have covered so far and how much more you have to do.

Unit F211		Unit F212		Unit F213
Cell, Exchange and Transport	+	Molecules, Biodiversity, Food and Health	+	Practical Skills in Biology 1

The specification outlines what you are expected to learn and do. The content of the specification is written as **learning outcomes**; these state what you should be able to do after studying and revising each topic. Some learning outcomes are very precise and cover just a small amount of factual information. Some are much broader; do not think that any two learning outcomes will take exactly the same length of time to cover in class or during revision. Some of the learning outcomes deal with practical biology — these are covered in the **Focus on practical skills** boxes. It is a good idea to write a glossary for the words in the learning outcomes; the examiners will expect you to know what they mean. This guide should help you to do this.

The unit test

The examination paper will be printed in a booklet, in which you will write all your answers. The paper will have five, six or seven questions, each divided into parts. These parts comprise several short-answer questions (no more than 4 or 5 marks each) and one question requiring an extended answer, for around 7 or 8 marks. The unit test has a total of 60 marks and lasts 60 minutes.

Command terms

You need to know how to respond to the various command terms used in the unit test. These are outlined below.

'Describe' and 'explain'

These do not mean the same thing. 'Describe' means give a straightforward account. You may be asked to describe something on the paper, such as a graph. You may have to describe a structure or 'tell a story', for example by writing out the sequence of events in the cardiac cycle. If you are describing what is shown in a graph or a table you can often gain marks by quoting the data. 'Explain' means give some *reasons* for why something happens. 'Explain how...' means that you should show the way something functions. 'Explain why...' is asking you to give reasons for something, such as an event or outcome.

'Name', 'identify' and 'state'

These all require a very concise answer, maybe just one word, a phrase or a sentence.

'Calculate' and 'determine'

Expect to be tested on your numeracy skills. For example, the examiner may ask you to calculate a rate of reaction, a percentage, a percentage change or the magnification of a drawing. 'Determine' means more than just calculate. You may be asked to explain how measurements should be taken and how a final answer is calculated, or asked how to determine the volume of air taken into the lungs during 1 minute, from data obtained with a spirometer (see p. 83 and p. 84 in the Questions and Answers Section).

'Outline'

This means give several different points about the topic without concentrating on one or giving lots of detail.

'Draw', 'sketch' and 'complete'

'Draw' and 'sketch' mean draw something on the examination paper, such as a sketch graph, a drawing or a diagram. 'Complete' means that there is something you need to finish, such as a table, diagram or graph. You will not be expected to draw a graph on the examination paper, but you may have to put a line on a pair of axes to show a relationship.

'Differences'

If you are asked to give some 'differences', then it is likely that you will be asked to say how 'A differs from B'. The examiners will assume that anything you write will be something about A that is not the same as for B. Sometimes the examiner will give you a table to complete to show differences and then ask you to write something about both A and B.

Prepare yourself

Make sure that you have two or more blue or black pens, a couple of sharp pencils (preferably HB), a ruler, an eraser, a pencil sharpener, a watch and a calculator.

When told to start the paper, look through all the questions. Find the end of the last question (sometimes it is on the back page and might be missed). Find and read the question that requires an extended answer. Some points may come to mind immediately — write them down before you forget.

There is no need to start by answering question 1, but the examiner will have set something straightforward to help calm your nerves. Look carefully at the number of marks available for each question. Do not write a lengthy answer if there are only 1 or 2 marks available. If you want to change an answer, cross it out and rewrite the answer clearly. Always write within the box printed on each page. If you write an answer or continue an answer somewhere other than on the allotted lines, indicate clearly where this is.

When you reach the question that requires an extended answer:
- plan what you intend to write and make sure it is in a logical sequence
- do not write out the question
- keep to the point — you do not need an introduction or a summary
- use diagrams or sketch graphs if they help your answer — remember to label and annotate them
- pay careful attention to spelling, punctuation and grammar

Time yourself. Work out where you expect to be after 25 minutes. Leave yourself at least 5 minutes to check your paper to make sure you have attempted all the questions and have left nothing out. The best way to do this is to check the mark allocation — have you offered something for each mark?

introduction

Content
Guidance

This Content Guidance section is a guide to the content of Unit F211: Cells, Exchange and Transport. The unit is divided into two modules.

Module 1: Cells. The sections of this module are:
- Cell structure
- Cell membranes
- Cell division, cell diversity and cellular organisation

Module 2: Exchange and Transport. The sections of this module are:
- Exchange surfaces and breathing
- Transport in animals
- Transport in plants

This section will help you to organise your notes and highlight the important points. The 'key facts' are presented as easy-to-remember 'chunks' of knowledge.

This section will also help you to understand the links with practical work. You may need knowledge of this unit when doing the practical tasks in Unit F213.

There is no Unit Guide in this series specifically for Unit F213. In this guide you will find references to the three tasks that you will undertake as part of the unit. They are:
- the **qualitative task**, e.g. carrying out an experiment that does not give you anything you can measure or determine, and which may involve recording colours or drawing from a microscope
- the **quantitative task**, e.g. carrying out a practical task in which you record measurements
- the **evaluative task**, e.g. commenting critically on the practical procedure and the results you obtained while doing the quantitative task

Finally, this guide will help you to understand how the key facts fit into the wider picture of biology — you need knowledge of this module to understand much of the content of the other AS unit. Unit F211 also supports the three units in the A2 course.

Units

Various units are used in this guide.

Length: nm, μm, mm, m and km; 1000 nm (nanometres) = 1 μm (micrometre); 1000 μm = 1 mm (millimetre); 1000 mm = 1 m; 1000 m = 1 km

You may be expected to find the measurements or magnifications of cells in Units F211 and F213.

Volume: cm^3 and dm^3; 1000 cm^3 = 1 dm^3

You will often find ml (millilitre) on glassware and in books. Examination papers, however, use cm^3 (cubic centimetre or 'centimetre cubed') and dm^3 (cubic decimetre or 'decimetre cubed'). 1 cm^3 is the same as 1 ml; 1 dm^3 is the same as 1 litre (1l or 1L). 1000 cm^3 = 1 dm^3.

You will come across volumes in the section on exchange surfaces and breathing and transport in animals, with such measurements as tidal volume, vital capacity, stroke volume and cardiac output.

Pressure: Pa (pascals) and kPa (kilopascals); 1000 Pa = 1 kPa

The medical profession uses millimetres of mercury (mmHg) for measuring blood pressure. Examination papers use kilopascals (kPa). 'Normal' blood pressure is often given as '120 over 80' or 120 mmHg (systolic) and 80 mmHg (diastolic). These are equivalent to 15.8 kPa and 10.5 kPa. See pp. 49–54 for more about this. Water potential is measured in pressure units (see pp. 25–26).

Module 1: Cells
Cell structure

Microscopy

Key concepts you must understand

Size matters

It is very difficult to imagine the range of sizes that biologists deal with. A blue whale can be as long as 30 m. The largest viruses are about 0.0004 mm. Many plant and animal cells are between 0.02 mm and 0.04 mm.

We use microscopes in biology because much of what we want to see is so small. Many cells, for example, are about 0.02 mm across. At best, our eyes can only make out things that are about 0.1 mm in size, so using our eyes alone we would never see structures inside cells. The light microscope (LM) uses a beam of light that is focused by means of glass lenses. The electron microscope (EM) uses a beam of electrons focused by magnetic lenses.

Units

The units to use for measuring microscopic structures are the micrometre (μm) and the nanometre (nm). Remember:
- to convert millimetres to micrometres, multiply by 1000
- to convert micrometres to nanometres, multiply by 1000

Also remember:
- 1 μm (micrometre) = 0.001 mm; 1000 μm = 1 mm
- 1 nm (nanometre) = 0.001μm; 1000 nm = 1 μm

Key facts you must know

Resolution is the ability to see detail. The LM has a resolution of 0.0002 mm. This means that two points this distance apart are viewed as separate objects. Visible light has a wavelength of between 400 nm and 700 nm. Objects about half the size of the wavelength interrupt the rays of light and are resolved in the LM. However, anything smaller than 0.0002 mm is not visible because it is too small to interrupt the light. No matter how much a photograph taken through the LM is enlarged, small cellular structures are never visible.

Magnification is the ratio between the actual size of an object and the size of an image, such as a photograph or a drawing.

content guidance

Examiners may ask you to calculate magnifications or actual sizes. You should use these formulae:

magnification = size of image/actual size

actual size = size of image/magnification

With the LM, some structures, such as mitochondria, are just visible.

Electron microscopes

The wavelength of an electron beam is about 1 nm, so objects half this size are visible. As the resolution is so good, the magnification can be very high (×250 000 or more). In the EM, magnets focus beams of electrons and an image is formed when the electrons strike a fluorescent screen or photographic film. The **transmission electron microscope (TEM)** is used to view thin sections of tissues. The **scanning electron microscope (SEM)** is used to view surfaces of three-dimensional objects, such as the bodies of insects and surfaces of cells.

Inside electron microscopes is a vacuum. This allows electrons to travel towards the specimen and afterwards strike a fluorescent screen or photographic film. It means, however, that living cells cannot be observed, since they would explode. In the light microscope, it is possible to watch living processes, such as cell division.

Characteristic	Light microscope	Electron microscope
Wavelength	400–700 nm	1.0 nm
Resolution	200 nm	0.5 nm
Useful magnification	up to ×1000 (at best ×1500)	up to ×100 000 in SEM up to ×250 000 in TEM

Table 1 The main characteristics of light and electron microscopes

Staining

Most biological material is colourless or transparent, and is composed of elements with low atomic mass. This means that visible light travels through tissues in the LM without being absorbed or reflected, so there is very little, if any, contrast. This problem is solved by adding stains, such as iodine, methylene blue and toluidine blue, all of which you may use during your course. Stains used in electron microscopy are salts of heavy metals, such as lead and uranium. These combine with proteins, for example in membranes, and absorb or scatter electrons as they pass through the specimen. This makes these areas show dark on photographs taken using the EM.

Links You may be asked to find the actual size of a cell or organelle in an electron micrograph or in a drawing made from an electron micrograph. Measure in millimetres, multiply by 1000 and divide by the given magnification to give an answer in micrometres (μm). You may also be asked to calculate the magnification of a cell or an organelle in an electron micrograph. You will be told the actual size in micrometres. Measure the size of the cell in millimetres, convert into micrometres by multiplying by 1000 and divide by the actual size. If you calculate a size, check it looks right. Here are some examples of things you may be asked: cells, 10–100 μm; chloroplasts, 3–10 μm; mitochondria, 1–3 μm; bacteria, 0.5–30 μm; membranes, 7–10 nm. If your answers are very different from these values, then you must have made a mistake. Sometimes you will be asked to give your answer to the nearest whole number, which means you may have to round your answer down or up.

Cell structure and function

Key facts you must know

Cell ultrastructure

The fine structure of cells that is visible with an electron microscope is often called **cell ultrastructure**. Many of the structures (**organelles**) in plant and animal cells, such as chloroplasts and mitochondria, are made of membranes. Within the cytoplasm of plant and animal cells are fibrous structures composed of protein, which form the **cytoskeleton**. These fibrous structures include microfilaments, made from the protein actin, and microtubules, made from tubulin. Cilia, undulipodia and centrioles are composed of microtubules. Ribosomes are made of protein and ribonucleic acid (RNA).

Animal and plant cells are **eukaryotic** because they have a nucleus and organelles.

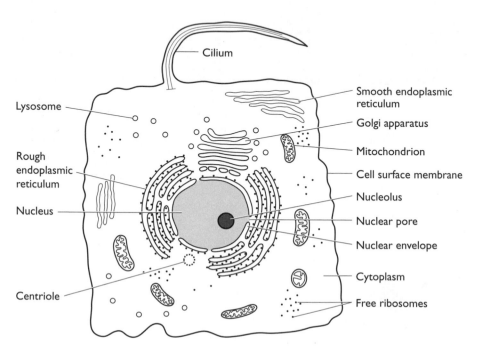

Figure 1 A generalised animal cell viewed with the electron microscope

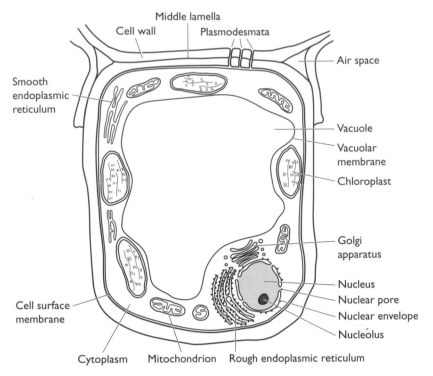

Figure 2 A generalised plant cell viewed with the electron microscope

Functions of cellular structures

Table 2 summarises the features and functions of the main cellular structures in animal and plant cells.

Cellular structures	Features	Function(s)
Rough endoplasmic reticulum (RER)	Flat sacs of membrane enclosing fluid-filled space; outer surface is covered in ribosomes	Ribosomes carry out protein synthesis; RER transports proteins to Golgi apparatus
Smooth endoplasmic reticulum (SER)	Like RER but with no ribosomes on outer surface	Makes triglycerides (fats), phospholipids, cholesterol
Golgi apparatus	Pile of flat sacs with vesicles forming around the edge	Modifies proteins by adding carbohydrates; packages proteins; makes lysosomes
Mitochondria (singular: mitochondrion)	Formed of two membranes surrounding a fluid-filled matrix; inner membrane is highly folded to give large surface area for enzymes of respiration	Site of aerobic respiration
Ribosomes	Attached to RER or free in cytoplasm — made of protein and RNA	Assemble amino acids to make proteins

Cellular structures	Features	Function(s)
Lysosomes	Single membrane surrounds fluid filled with enzymes	Contain enzymes for destroying worn out parts of cell and for digesting food particles
Chloroplasts	Many internal membranes, giving large surface area for chlorophyll, other pigments and enzymes of photosynthesis	Site of all the reactions of photosynthesis
Plasma (cell surface) membrane	Several (see pp. 19–20 for details)	Controls entry and exit of materials; retains cell contents
Nuclear envelope	Structure like that of ER, with ribosomes on outer surface; pores to allow substances to pass between cytoplasm and nucleus	Separates nucleus from cytoplasm
Nucleus	Clearly visible in LM and EM when stained	Contains genetic information as DNA in chromosomes
Nucleolus	Darkly staining area in nucleus	Produces ribosomes
Microfilaments	Made of actin — a type of protein	Provide mechanical support for cells; part of the cytoskeleton
Microtubules	Made of tubulin — a type of protein formed into hollow tubes	Part of the cytoskeleton; provide pathways within cells to enable vesicles and organelles to move about within the cytoplasm; form cilia, undulipodia and centrioles; form the spindle to move chromosomes during anaphase of nuclear division
Cilia (singular: cilium)	Extend from cell surface; made of microtubules arranged into a '9+2' arrangement in the shaft (9 peripheral microtubules and 2 central ones); no central microtubules in the base; extend from cell surface; surrounded by plasma membrane	Found in large groups; move fluid or mucus past cells (e.g. in the trachea); move eggs along the fallopian tube
Undulipodia (singular: undulipodium)	As for cilia	Found singly to move individual cells, e.g. sperm in animals and in some plants, such as ferns and mosses
Centrioles	Made of microtubules in same arrangement as in base of a cilium; not found in flowering plants	Assemble the spindle to move chromosomes when nuclei divide in animal cells (see pp. 28–29)

Table 2 Sub-cellular structures found in animal and plant cells

Key concepts you must understand

The cells depicted in Figures 1 and 2 are 'generalised' cells. They do not exist! They are drawn to show all the structures in plant and animal cells. You should look carefully at photographs taken through the light microscope (these are known as photomicrographs, or PMs) to see the differences between plant and animal cells. Sometimes you will be expected to identify organelles from electron micrographs (EMs) or from drawings made from electron micrographs. You should become proficient at recognising the organelles and using this information to explain how the structure of a cell, such as a sperm cell or a guard cell, is related to its function. There are many examples of how to do this throughout this Unit Guide and in the one for Unit F212.

Links Aspects of cell structure and function occur throughout the AS course. For example, in Module 2 of this unit you will study red blood cells and how they carry oxygen and carbon dioxide. In Module 2 of Unit F212 you will study the action of phagocytes and lymphocytes in defence against disease-causing organisms. You should look at PMs and EMs of these cells and relate structure to function.

You should also look at the function of organelles. Some of the organelles in Table 2 on pp. 15–16 are involved in the production of protein. Figure 1 in Question 1 on p. 73 shows you how the nucleus, RER, Golgi apparatus and secretory vesicles work together to make and secrete a protein.

Prokaryotes

Key facts you must know

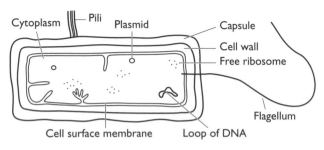

Figure 3 A generalised prokaryotic cell

Prokaryotic cells do not have a nucleus and have no organelles made of membranes. Most are smaller than eukaryotic cells.

Structures shared with eukaryotic cells	Cytoplasm; ribosomes; cell surface membrane
Structures from eukaryotic cells never found in prokaryotic cells	Nucleus; nucleolus; nuclear envelope; mitochondria; Golgi apparatus; chloroplasts; cilia; vacuoles
Structures only found in prokaryotic cells	Ring of DNA (sometimes called bacterial chromosome)
Structures found in some prokaryotic cells	Small rings of DNA known as plasmids; pili (small projections from the surface); slimy outer capsule; flagellum (not built of microtubules)

Table 3 A summary of the differences and similarities between eukaryotic and prokaryotic cells

Links Every time you come across cells of different types, check to see if they are eukaryotic or prokaryotic. When you study infectious diseases in Module 2 of Unit F212, you will find that the parasitic organism that causes malaria is eukaryotic; the organism that causes tuberculosis is a bacterium and therefore prokaryotic. You could identify the differences between prokaryotic and eukaryotic cells, as well as those between animal and plant cells, and summarise them in a table such as the one below:

Feature	Prokaryotic cell	Eukaryotic cell	
		Plant cell	Animal cell

Cell membranes

Fluid mosaic structure of membranes

Key concepts you must understand

Membranes form boundaries and divide cells into compartments. The cell membrane (also known as the plasma membrane or cell surface membrane) forms the outermost boundary of the cell. This allows cells to be different from their external environment. Membranes keep in large molecules such as enzymes, RNA and DNA. They keep out many others. They are barriers between the cytoplasm and the outside world. But cells need to exchange substances with their surroundings, so membranes are permeable — not freely permeable to anything and everything, but **partially permeable** to some substances.

Organelles, for example mitochondria, chloroplasts, endoplasmic reticulum and Golgi apparatus, are made of membranes and are separate compartments within cells. For example, the lysosome membrane encloses enzymes and stops them breaking down molecules, such as proteins, in the cytoplasm.

Key facts you must know

All membranes have the same basic structure — the fluid mosaic structure.

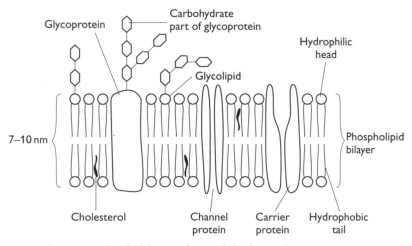

Figure 4 The fluid mosaic model of membrane structure

Figure 4 shows a cross-section of a tiny part of a membrane. It is composed of a double layer (bilayer) of phospholipids, together with proteins. Each phospholipid molecule has a 'head' and two 'tails'. The head end is polar and 'water-loving' (hydrophilic). The tails are non-polar and 'water-hating' (hydrophobic). Phospholipid heads are soluble in water; the tails provide a hydrophobic barrier that many water-soluble substances cannot cross easily. This hydrophobic barrier restricts the movement of substances in and out of cells, so helping to keep a constant environment inside the cytoplasm.

How are the components arranged?

Phospholipids

- Membranes have two layers of phospholipid, forming a bilayer.
- The molecules in the two layers have opposite orientations, so that the non-polar ends associate with each other and the polar ends face the cytoplasm and the fluid outside the cell.

Proteins

- Membrane proteins are embedded in the phospholipid bilayer. Transmembrane proteins extend right through the bilayer with one end in the cytoplasm and the other end extending to the outside.
- Transmembrane proteins are held in the membrane because they have hydrophobic regions that span the hydrophobic interior of the membrane.

Carbohydrates

- These are short chains of sugar molecules that branch to give 'tree-like' attachments to proteins and lipids.
- Glycolipids are lipids with chains of sugar molecules attached.
- Glycoproteins are proteins with chains of sugar molecules attached.
- Carbohydrates are attached to lipids and proteins only on the external surfaces of cell membranes.

Cholesterol

- These molecules have polar and non-polar regions. Polar regions bind to polar heads of phospholipids; non-polar regions bind to phospholipid tails.
- It maintains the stability of membranes by preventing phospholipids solidifying at low temperatures and becoming too fluid at high temperatures.
- Cholesterol reduces the permeability of membranes to water, ions and polar molecules.
- It is not found in the membranes of prokaryotes.

Why fluid mosaic?

Fluid

The membrane is held together mainly by hydrophobic interactions between the phospholipids and between proteins and phospholipids. These weak interactions allow the molecules to move so that the membrane is liquid. Phospholipid molecules move in the plane of the membrane. Proteins are much larger and move more slowly — imagine protein molecules moving about like icebergs in a 'sea' of lipid.

Mosaic

A membrane is like a collage of many different proteins in the lipid bilayer. Think of a Roman mosaic made of tiny pieces of tile. Now think of the pieces constantly moving about and you should have a picture in your mind of a fluid mosaic.

Cell signalling

Many glycoproteins are receptors for chemical signals sent between cells. You will remember from GCSE that neurones (nerve cells) release chemicals into gaps known as synapses. These chemicals act as signals from one neurone to the next, so that information can be sent through the nervous system. As another way of signalling, some cells release hormones into the bloodstream.

When tissues are damaged, special cells called mast cells release histamine, which signals to cells lining blood capillaries to become leaky and allow more fluid to pass out from the blood.

The cells that receive such signals are called target cells, and they have receptors on the surface of their membranes that bind with the signalling molecule. The shape of the receptor matches the shape of the signalling molecule, so the two fit together. It is possible to design drugs to bind to these receptors. For example, some asthmatics use salbutamol (Ventolin™) in an inhaler. This drug binds to receptors for adrenaline on smooth muscle in the bronchioles, making these air passages widen, thereby making it easier to breathe.

Links Membranes are involved in all exchanges between living things and their environment, for example, across alveoli in the lungs (see p. 40) and across plant root hairs (see pp. 66–67). You will need to know the structure of membranes if you are asked to explain the effect of different temperatures on membrane permeability (see 'Focus on practical skills' below).

Cholesterol is a molecule that we need, but also one that can cause harm (see Module 2 of Unit F212 for more detail).

Cell signalling is a theme that recurs throughout the AS course and at A2. Note the importance of glycoprotein receptors as the 'receivers' on the target cells. Another theme that recurs throughout the course is that of protein shapes. Receptors and signalling molecules fit together because they have complementary shapes, in the same way that substrates and enzymes fit together.

Focus on practical skills: investigating membranes

The effect of temperature on membrane permeability

Some plant cells have vacuoles that contain pigments. Beetroot is a good example — the vacuoles contain the red pigment betalain. If you cut up a beetroot into small slices, you will notice that a lot of the red pigment leaks out, because you have cut through many cells. If you wash the slices of beetroot in lots of water the leakage will eventually stop because cell surface membranes and membranes around vacuoles in undamaged cells are intact. To investigate the effect of temperature on membranes, place some of the beetroot slices into test tubes of water, and place these into water baths at different temperatures. Leave them for a while, before pouring off the water and examining its appearance.

This investigation could be the subject of the qualitative task in Unit F213, e.g. you could compare the intensity of the colours in the test tubes and rank them. It is unlikely that any pigment will leak from beetroot tissue kept at 20°C, but a lot will leak when the tissue is immersed in water at 80°C or above. You could investigate whether there is a relationship between temperature and the quantity of pigment that leaks from the beetroot tissue.

This investigation could also be used for the quantitative task, but you would need a device that measures the intensity of colour in the test tubes, e.g. a colorimeter (described in the Unit Guide for Unit F212).

Why does temperature have this effect? At temperatures above 40°C, the membrane proteins will lose their structure — they will become denatured — which is something you have learnt at GCSE. The phospholipids will also gain more kinetic energy and the membrane will become more fluid. This happens to such an extent that the membrane breaks down and the pigment molecules can leak out.

Movement across membranes

Key concepts you must understand

Membranes are barriers, but they allow considerable exchange of substances between the cytoplasm and the surroundings. Some substances are small enough to pass through membranes easily; others are larger and need special methods. Some molecules move through the membrane down a concentration gradient, e.g. oxygen moves into animal cells and carbon dioxide diffuses out of animal cells in this way. This is **passive transport**, because the cell does not use any of its energy from respiration to move the molecules. All cells have a *lower* concentration of sodium ions than their surroundings, because they use membrane proteins to pump sodium ions out of the cells, utilising some of their energy to do this. This type of movement is **active transport**. Some molecules, and even large particles, are moved into or out of cells surrounded by membrane. This type of movement is **bulk transport**, and also requires energy from the cell to move vacuoles or small vesicles away from or towards the cell surface membrane.

Key facts you must know

There are five ways in which substances can cross membranes, divided into two categories:

Passive transport — not requiring energy from cells
- simple diffusion
- facilitated diffusion
- osmosis

content guidance

Transport mechanisms requiring energy from cells
- active transport
- bulk transport (endocytosis and exocytosis)

Simple diffusion

Non-polar molecules, such as steroid hormones, lipid-soluble vitamins (e.g. vitamins A and D), many narcotics, the respiratory gases oxygen and carbon dioxide, and small polar molecules such as water and urea, move through the phospholipid bilayer down their concentration gradients. This is a passive process. Ions and large polar molecules, such as sugars, cannot diffuse across membranes in this way.

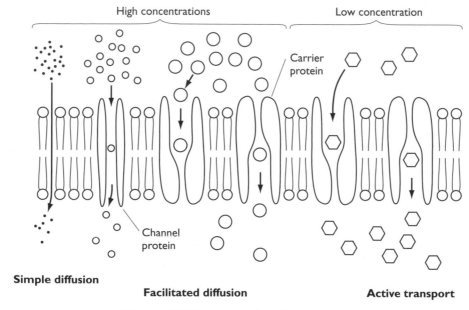

Figure 5 Diffusion and active transport

Facilitated diffusion

Proteins play a key role in regulating transport across membranes. **Channel proteins** each have a hollow core, which acts as a water-filled channel or pore. This allows small, polar molecules and ions to diffuse across membranes. This is known as facilitated diffusion because the channels allow this to happen (facilitate = make easier).

Carrier proteins work by binding to the substance and physically moving it across. The binding causes a change in the shape of the carrier and results in the bound substance being released at the other side of the membrane. This is also a type of facilitated diffusion when the substances involved move down their concentration gradients.

Osmosis

Osmosis is the diffusion of water across membranes. Water diffuses through the phospholipid bilayer and through special channel proteins, known as aquaporins. The direction in which water diffuses depends on water potential gradients, which are determined partly by the solute concentration in the cytoplasm and the external surroundings, and partly by other factors, for example the pressure exerted by plant cell walls on the cytoplasm and vacuole. For more information about osmosis and water potential, see 'Focus on practical skills' on pp. 25–26.

Active transport

Active transport involves carrier proteins. Cells use energy to move substances from a low to a high concentration (against a concentration gradient). As mentioned on p. 22, many cells use active transport to move sodium ions out of the cytoplasm in exchange for potassium ions — the 'sodium pump'. This helps regulate their volume, as three sodium ions are pumped out for every two potassium ions pumped in. Removing sodium ions helps to prevent the cell water potential falling very low and too much water diffusing in by osmosis.

Bulk transport

Bulk transport is used for the transport of larger molecules and particles. Exocytosis and endocytosis (pinocytosis and phagocytosis) are examples.

Exocytosis

Substances are moved out of cells. Vesicles travel towards the cell surface and fuse with the membrane to extrude substances. For example, this happens in pancreatic cells that secrete enzymes to digest food in the small intestine.

Endocytosis

Substances are brought into cells. Vesicles form at the cell surface and move into the cell, e.g. when phagocytes engulf bacteria. Phagocytosis is the uptake of particles from the surroundings; pinocytosis is the uptake of liquids.

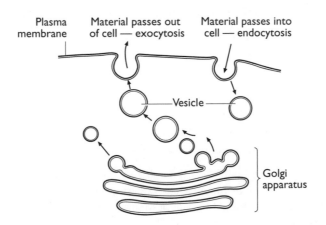

Figure 6 Bulk transport

Focus on practical skills: osmosis

Put some plant tissue — e.g. slices of courgette, aubergine or whole pickled onions — into some concentrated salt solution. After a short period of time (minutes in the case of aubergine), the tissue will feel much softer, because water has diffused out of the cells by osmosis. Cut some more slices and put them into distilled water. After a while the tissues will feel firmer because water has diffused into the cells by osmosis.

Osmosis is a good topic for the quantitative task in Unit F213. Vegetables such as potato, swede or celeriac can also be used. Make up a range of sucrose solutions, starting with a 1 mol dm^{-3} (1 molar) solution (put 34.2 grams of sucrose in a beaker; add about 80 cm^3 of warm distilled water; stir until the sucrose is dissolved and then add enough distilled water to make the final volume of your solution up to 100 cm^3). Follow the procedure shown in Figure 7 to make solutions with different concentrations. The total volume of each concentration is 10 cm^3. If this is not enough, double the volumes shown to make 20 cm^3 of each concentration.

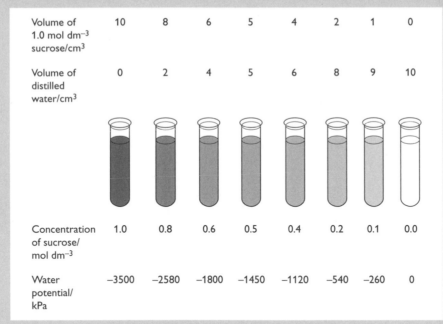

Volume of 1.0 mol dm^{-3} sucrose/cm^3	10	8	6	5	4	2	1	0
Volume of distilled water/cm^3	0	2	4	5	6	8	9	10
Concentration of sucrose/ mol dm^{-3}	1.0	0.8	0.6	0.5	0.4	0.2	0.1	0.0
Water potential/ kPa	−3500	−2580	−1800	−1450	−1120	−540	−260	0

Figure 7 Making some solutions of sucrose

Cut the plant tissue into pieces of equal size and shape. Dry the pieces with filter paper or paper towels and weigh them. Put each piece into a different solution and leave for at least 12 hours. Take the pieces out of solution, blot dry and reweigh. By finding the change in mass you will obtain some **quantitative**

results. Because all the pieces are unlikely to be *exactly* the same mass when you start the experiment, calculate the percentage change in mass:

$$\text{percentage change in mass} = \frac{\text{change in mass}}{\text{original mass}} \times 100$$

Plot the results on a graph. Water potential in kPa is the independent variable, so should be placed on the horizontal axis. Some pieces of tissue will have gained in mass, because the water potential of the bathing solution was *higher* than the water potential of the cells in the tissue. Some pieces will have lost mass, because the water potential of the bathing solution was *lower* than the water potential of the cells in the tissue. If there is a solution in which the pieces did not change mass, that solution has the same water potential as the cells. It is unlikely that you will find this, but you can use an intercept on your graph to find the water potential which would give no change in mass.

A quantitative task such as this will be the subject of the evaluative task in Unit F213. Read through the procedure above and make some critical comments about aspects such as reliability, validity and accuracy.

The water potential of pure water is 0 kPa. When a solute is added to water, the water potential decreases. If a pressure is exerted on a solution (for example by the cell wall withstanding the expansion of a vacuole that is filling with water), the water potential increases. Remember that water always diffuses by osmosis *down* a water potential gradient.

It is not possible to complete this sort of investigation with animal cells. When immersed in solutions with a high water potential, so much water enters by osmosis that the cells fill up and burst because they have no cell wall. It is possible to show this happening to red blood cells by adding a drop of blood to some distilled water. The cells burst immediately, releasing haemoglobin to give a clear, red solution. However, if you put a drop of blood into a 0.9% sodium chloride solution, you see a cloudy red suspension. The red blood cells remain intact, because the sodium chloride solution has the same water potential as the blood plasma in which red blood cells are suspended. If you put red blood cells into a 1.5% sodium chloride solution, you again see a cloudy suspension, but if you look at the cells under a microscope you will see that they have a crinkly outline. This is because water has diffused out of the cells by osmosis and the cells have shrunk. The 1.5% solution has a *lower* water potential than blood plasma and the cells.

Cell division, cell diversity and cellular organisation

Key concepts you must understand

The cell cycle

Multicellular organisms, such as animals and plants, grow in two basic ways: the cells increase in size and they divide. Cells increase in size by making new molecules, such as phospholipids and proteins, new membranes and new organelles. Cells cannot grow like this indefinitely. When they reach a certain size, diffusion distances between the cell surface membrane and the centre of the cell become too great and not enough oxygen reaches the mitochondria for respiration. Also, there is not a large enough surface for sufficient diffusion of oxygen and carbon dioxide relative to the size of the cell (see p. 37). Before these problems arise, a cell divides into two daughter cells.

Stem cells are found throughout the bodies of animals, although they are often concentrated in areas such as the skin, the lining of the gut and the bone marrow (where they produce replacement cells). In plants, **meristematic cells** retain the ability to grow and divide and are the equivalent of stem cells. Meristems are areas where these cells are found, including root tips, shoot tips and the cambium that gives rise to xylem and phloem tissues.

The cell cycle shows the different stages of a cell's life.

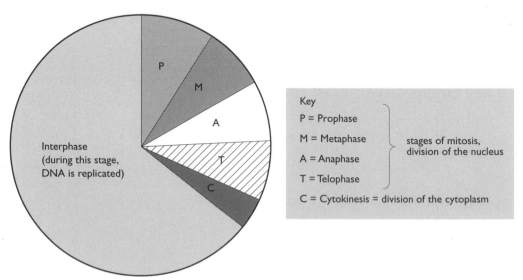

Figure 8 The stages of the cell cycle. Mitosis (PMAT) takes up about 5–10%, which is too short a time to show clearly on this diagram.

During interphase, cells make new membrane and organelles, store energy and grow larger. They also make new DNA and check that it does not have any errors (for more information, see Unit F212). Mitosis is the division of the nucleus, and this is usually followed by division of the cytoplasm.

Key facts you must know

Animals repair themselves following wounding or natural processes such as giving birth. Plants also repair themselves after wounding, for example when they are damaged by storms. New cells are produced in much the same way as during growth.

Some animals and plants reproduce asexually, by budding or growing parts that separate from the parent. Asexual reproduction is really just a form of growth, so it also involves mitosis. For example, yeast reproduces asexually by budding. When a yeast cell reaches a certain size, part of the cell bulges out to form a bud. The nucleus divides in a way similar to that shown in Figure 9, but the nuclear envelope remains intact during the process. After the nucleus has divided, the bud may separate from the parent cell.

The daughter cells produced by mitosis have the same genetic information as the parent cell because all the cells have the same DNA. They are *genetically* identical. This makes it possible for cells to function together as one unit even if the daughter cells *express* different genes and function differently. New individuals produced by asexual reproduction are therefore genetically identical to the parent and are likely to survive in the same environment as the parent. This is especially the case with plants that spread by asexual reproduction, such as bluebells growing in a wood.

Mitosis

Key concepts you must understand

Chromosomes are made of DNA and protein. DNA is the important molecule because it codes for all the features of an organism. The proteins in chromosomes help with DNA packing. DNA is a long molecule, wound around proteins to make chromosomes. When you look at a dividing cell through a microscope, you can see chromosomes if they have been stained. Sometimes it is possible to see separate chromosomes, especially at metaphase during mitosis.

Key facts you must know

During interphase of the cell cycle, DNA replication occurs, so that each chromosome has two identical DNA molecules. These are wound around proteins to form chromatids — joined together at the centromere. Now there are two copies of each molecule of DNA within one chromosome. At the start of anaphase, the DNA at the centromere separates so that the sister chromatids come apart. During anaphase, the sister chromatids move to opposite ends of the cell. They are pulled by the microtubules that make up the spindle. At telophase, they form two nuclei with identical genetic information and the same number of chromosomes as the original cell. Plant cells do not have centrioles to organise the microtubules into a spindle, and they divide by forming a new cell wall to separate the daughter cells. Prokaryotes do not divide by mitosis. The stages of mitosis in an animal cell are outlined in Figure 9.

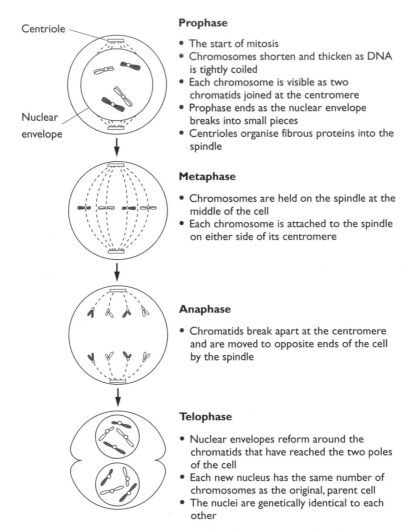

Centriole

Nuclear envelope

Prophase

- The start of mitosis
- Chromosomes shorten and thicken as DNA is tightly coiled
- Each chromosome is visible as two chromatids joined at the centromere
- Prophase ends as the nuclear envelope breaks into small pieces
- Centrioles organise fibrous proteins into the spindle

Metaphase

- Chromosomes are held on the spindle at the middle of the cell
- Each chromosome is attached to the spindle on either side of its centromere

Anaphase

- Chromatids break apart at the centromere and are moved to opposite ends of the cell by the spindle

Telophase

- Nuclear envelopes reform around the chromatids that have reached the two poles of the cell
- Each new nucleus has the same number of chromosomes as the original, parent cell
- The nuclei are genetically identical to each other

Figure 9 Stages of mitosis in an animal cell

Links Replication of DNA must occur before mitosis. Each chromosome must have two DNA molecules so that they can be divided between the two new cells. More information on replication is provided in Unit F212. The best way to understand the events that occur in mitosis is to watch a time-lapse film of a cell dividing. You can find some animations of mitosis at:

   www.biology.arizona.edu/cell_bio/tutorials/cell_cycle/main.html.

You should study the stages of mitosis in a root tip preparation. You may be given a prepared microscope slide or you may prepare one yourself — see Student Sheet No. 17 on the Science and Plants for Schools website:

   www-saps.plantsci.cam.ac.uk

You may be expected to make annotated drawings of the stages of the cell cycle. Do not draw something like Figure 9, which is a *diagram*. You should draw what you see and use annotations to describe the appearance of the chromosomes and state what they are doing at each stage. A good way to remember the sequence of stages in mitosis is 'PMAT'.

Chromosomes and life cycles

Key concepts you must understand

Diploid cells have two sets of chromosomes. This means there are two chromosomes of each type. In humans, the diploid number is 46; there are 23 pairs of chromosomes. We inherit our chromosomes from our parents. One set of chromosomes is inherited from our father, one from our mother. So one chromosome of each type is paternal and the other is maternal in origin. Think about the sex chromosomes, X and Y, in boys. Males have one X and one Y. A boy inherits his X chromosome from his mother and his Y chromosome from his father. In the same way, he inherits one of each pair of chromosomes from his father and the other from his mother. Each pair of chromosomes is known as an homologous pair.

Key facts you must know

Homologous chromosomes have the same:
- shape and size
- position of the centromere
- genes

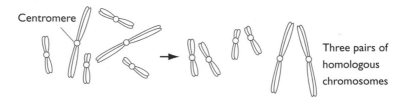

Figure 10 Homologous chromosomes

It is possible to see homologous pairs of chromosomes under the microscope. Computers can scan photographs of cells taken at metaphase of mitosis. They look for similarities, particularly in the banding patterns that chromosomes have when treated with certain dyes. The images of the chromosomes are then put into pairs.

During sexual reproduction, gametes (sex cells) fuse at fertilisation. From generation to generation, the diploid number remains constant. There is no doubling of the chromosome number with each generation, as this would lead to cells with huge numbers of chromosomes and very large quantities of DNA. The diploid number stays constant from generation to generation because the number of chromosomes in gametes is half the diploid number. Meiosis is the type of nuclear division that halves the chromosome number. It is sometimes called a reduction division because of this.

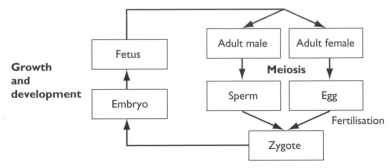

Figure 11 The position of meiosis in the human life cycle

Differentiation

Figure 8 on p. 27 suggests that cells continue dividing throughout their lives. Some cells remain able to do this — in animals these are tissue stem cells that produce new cells to replace those which have worn out or died. Stem cells in bone marrow produce new red and white blood cells throughout their life. Cells destined to become red blood cells (erythrocytes) go through a series of changes:

- Ribosomes make many molecules of haemoglobin.
- Mitochondria and other organelles disintegrate.
- The nucleus is extruded.

Differentiation is the term used to describe these changes, which a cell goes through as it becomes specialised to carry out its specific function(s). For example, some white blood cells search out and engulf bacteria. These are known as neutrophils and they differentiate in bone marrow:

- Ribosomes make enzymes, which are packaged by the Golgi apparatus in lysosomes.
- The nucleus changes shape to become lobed — this allows neutrophils to move through the walls of blood capillaries.

In plants, meristematic cells in the cambium produce xylem and phloem cells (see p. 65). In many trees and shrubs, the cambium produces new xylem during the growing season to give the familiar growth rings that you see in branches and tree trunks when they are cut in section.

Links You will learn the details of meiosis at A2. For now, remember that meiosis halves the chromosome number and occurs in life cycles with sexual reproduction.

Tissues, organs and organ systems

Key concepts you must understand

Biologists often talk about **levels of organisation**. Organelles carry out different functions in cells. This is the cell level of organisation. At the tissue level, similar cells cooperate to perform one or several functions. In organs, different tissues work together to perform a variety of major functions. In an organ system, organs work together to carry out major functions for the body, such as digestion, excretion and breathing.

Key facts you must know

Multicellular animals and plants are made up of large numbers of cells. Tissues are made of many cells that perform one or several functions. Often the cells are all of the same type. For example, epithelia are sheets of cells that line organs in the body and separate internal tissues from air, blood, food or waste that travel through tubes in the body. The outer part of your skin is an epithelium made of several layers of cells.

Animal tissues

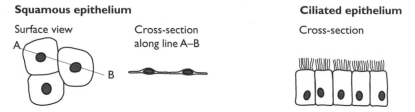

Figure 12 Squamous epithelium and ciliated epithelium

Cells forming squamous epithelia are flat and very thin. Looked at from above, each cell resembles a fried egg, with the nucleus projecting like a yolk. Single layers of squamous epithelia, such as those lining the alveoli, are thin to help diffusion.

Ciliated epithelial cells, such as those lining the airways in the lungs, have many cilia to move fluid or mucus over the surface. The cells have many mitochondria to provide energy for the cilia to beat.

Plant tissues

Xylem and phloem are the transport tissues of plants. Both are composed of three types of cell:

- Cells that form tubes to provide a transport pathway.

- Parenchyma cells for storage and energy provision.
- Fibres to help provide support.

The transport cells in xylem are **vessel elements**. As these develop, they gain a strong, thickened cell wall and lose their cytoplasm, so becoming rigid and empty. They also lose their end walls, so they form a continuous column of cells, known as a **xylem vessel**, which has little resistance to the flow of water.

The transport cells in phloem are **sieve tube elements**. These do not become thick-walled and they keep some of their cytoplasm. The end walls are perforated to form sieve plates. Sieve tube elements form continuous columns known as **sieve tubes** for the transport of soluble substances, such as sucrose and amino acids, throughout the plant.

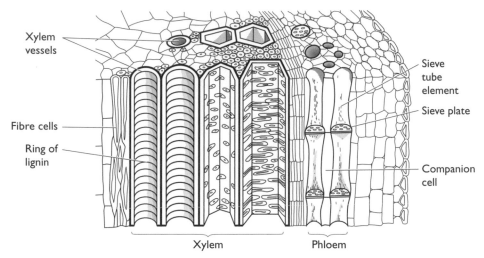

Figure 13 Transport pathways in a plant stem: xylem vessels and phloem sieve tubes in transverse section and in longitudinal section

Organs

The human body has a number of different organs, such as heart, lungs, stomach, pancreas, spleen, brain, kidneys and liver. Examples of plant organs are leaf, stem and root. Organs are structures made of several tissues that work together to carry out a number of functions. The leaf contains: epidermis for protection, parenchyma for photosynthesis and storage, xylem for transport of water, phloem for transport of sucrose.

Organ systems

Organs work together to carry out certain functions for animals. For example, in the digestive system of a mammal, the mouth, oesophagus, stomach, small and large intestines, liver, gall bladder and pancreas work together to digest and absorb food and eliminate all the undigested material.

Links Ciliated epithelia line the airways in the lungs and often occur with goblet cells (see pp. 39–40 for more information). Alveoli are lined by squamous epithelia (see p. 40). You could make a table of the major organ systems of the human body, listing the organs in each system, the tissues which comprise each organ, as well as the cell types. Use the following headings for your table:

Organ system	Organs	Tissues	Cell types

Focus on practical skills: making drawings from the microscope

Before you start the task, look at the slide with the naked eye before putting it on the microscope. This may help you position it on the stage of the microscope.

When you make a drawing, follow these simple rules:

- Low-power plans (e.g. of a leaf) only show the outlines of the tissues — they do not include drawings of cells.
- High-power drawings should show a small number of cells (three or four maximum) and they should be drawn a reasonable size so you can show any detail inside them.
- Use a sharp HB pencil and draw single lines.
- Do not use any shading.
- Add labels and annotations (notes) to your drawing. Use a ruler to draw straight lines from the drawing to your labels and notes.

Figure 14 is a photograph of a leaf. Figure 15 is a low-power plan drawn from a slide and Figure 16 is a drawing of three palisade mesophyll cells as seen under high power.

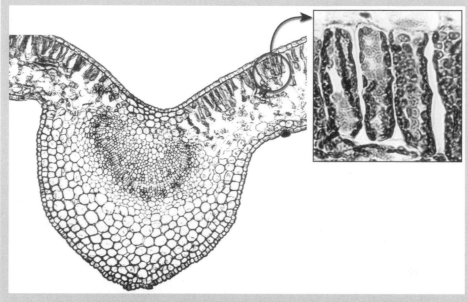

Figure 14 A cross-section of a leaf of privet. Inset shows some palisade mesophyll cells as seen with the high power of the microscope

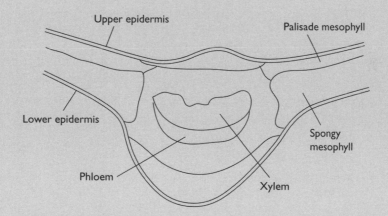

Figure 15 A tissue map drawn from a slide of a leaf similar to that shown in Figure 14

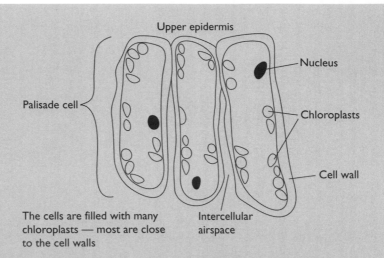

Figure 16 A high-power drawing of three palisade mesophyll cells from Figure 14

Annotations may be used to explain how the palisade cell is adapted to its functions. Palisade cells carry out most of the photosynthesis in this leaf, so you could mention:

- many chloroplasts to absorb light
- cells arranged at right angles to the surface of the leaf so light passes through the cell without being reflected by the cell walls
- large surface area exposed to air spaces for gas exchange

Module 2: Exchange and Transport
Exchange surfaces and breathing

Key concepts you must understand

Humans are large multicellular organisms. Although there are many organisms much larger than us, there are a vast number that are smaller. Size is important when it comes to exchanging substances, especially oxygen and carbon dioxide, with the surroundings and then moving them around the body. Figure 17 shows *Amoeba*, a small organism with a body consisting of one mass of cytoplasm. It is an example of a unicellular (one-celled) organism. *Amoeba* is non-photosynthetic and gains its energy by eating smaller organisms, such as bacteria. It lives in fresh water. Figure 17 also shows the exchange of gases that occurs between *Amoeba* and its surroundings. The cell surface membrane serves as the site of gaseous exchange, and its surface area is large enough to provide sufficient oxygen for respiration and for the removal of carbon dioxide.

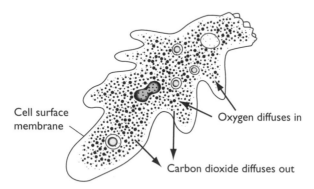

Cell surface membrane

Oxygen diffuses in

Carbon dioxide diffuses out

Figure 17 Amoeba is a unicellular organism that has a large surface area to volume ratio: it uses its body surface for gaseous exchange

Larger multicellular animals such as fish, insects and squid do not have sufficient body surface to act as the site of gaseous exchange, because there is not enough surface to absorb the oxygen required. This is why animals have lungs or gills with large surface areas as sites of gaseous exchange. There are also specialised surfaces for exchange elsewhere in the body; for example, the lining of the gut has a large surface area for the absorption of digested food.

It is difficult to calculate the surface area of animals and plants, but you need to know about how the **ratio** of surface area to volume changes as organisms increase in size. It helps to use cubes of different sizes to understand this principle. Table 4 shows what happens to the surface area to volume ratio as a cube increases in size.

Side/mm	1	2	3
Surface area/mm^2	$(1 \times 1 \times 6) = 6$	$(2 \times 2 \times 6) = 24$	$(3 \times 3 \times 6) = 54$
Volume/mm^3	$(1 \times 1 \times 1) = 1$	$(2 \times 2 \times 2) = 8$	$(3 \times 3 \times 3) = 27$
Surface area:volume ratio	6:1	3:1	2:1

Table 4

- Small organisms have a large surface area to volume ratio.
- Large organisms have a small surface area to volume ratio.
- Small organisms use their body surface for gaseous exchange, but larger organisms have specialised surfaces for exchange, e.g. gills and lungs.

Links Most examination papers in biology have questions that involve a calculation, so you may have to calculate surface area to volume ratios. To do this, divide the surface area by the volume — the resulting figure will represent how much surface area (in units of area, e.g. mm^2) there is for every unit of volume, e.g. for every 1 mm^3. Write this down as a ratio, for example A:1, where A is the number on your calculator. You may not get a whole number. If this is the case, round up or down to 1 decimal place. It is acceptable to write a surface area to volume ratio as something like 1.5:1.

You will meet the principle of *large surface area* many times in biology. Animal cells have microvilli to increase their surface area for exchange. Some relatively large organisms, such as jellyfish, make use of their surface for gaseous exchange. They have a large surface area to volume ratio because their bodies are extended into tentacles and they do not have any deep tissue — their bodies are made of two layers of cells.

Exchange in the mammalian lungs

Key concepts you must understand

Figure 18 shows the structure of the gaseous exchange system, consisting of the trachea and lungs.

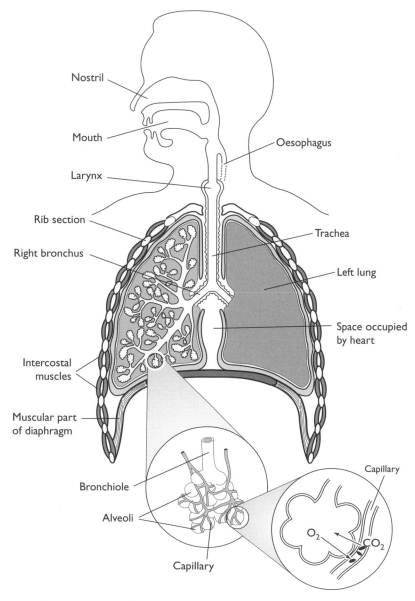

Figure 18 The gaseous exchange system, with details of the gaseous exchange surface formed by alveoli

(a)

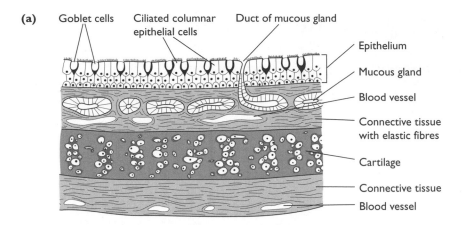

Goblet cells   Ciliated columnar   Duct of mucous gland
                epithelial cells

Epithelium

Mucous gland

Blood vessel

Connective tissue
with elastic fibres

Cartilage

Connective tissue

Blood vessel

(b)

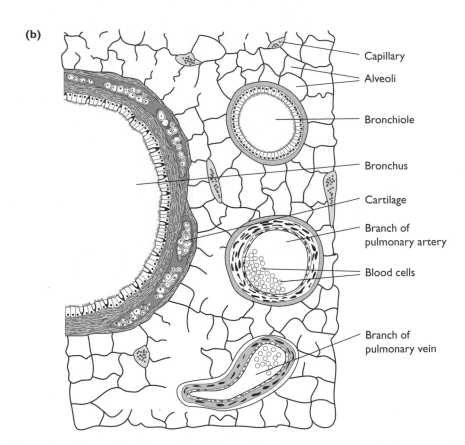

Capillary

Alveoli

Bronchiole

Bronchus

Cartilage

Branch of
pulmonary artery

Blood cells

Branch of
pulmonary vein

Figure 19 (a) Detail of the wall of the trachea (b) Distribution of tissues in the lungs

You should be clear about three different aspects of the gaseous exchange system:

- ventilation — breathing air in and out of the lungs
- gaseous exchange — diffusion of oxygen and carbon dioxide between air in the alveoli and the blood
- respiration — chemical processes that occur inside cells to transfer energy from molecules, such as glucose and fat, to ATP; may be aerobic or anaerobic

Ventilation and gaseous exchange occur to provide cells with oxygen and remove the carbon dioxide that they produce.

Structure	Distribution in gaseous exchange system	Functions
Ciliated epithelium	Trachea, bronchi, bronchioles	Cilia move mucus up the airways
Goblet cells	Trachea, bronchi	Secrete mucus
Cartilage	Trachea, bronchi	Holds open the airways to allow easy flow of air
Smooth muscle	Trachea, bronchi and bronchioles	Contracts to narrow the airways
Elastic fibres	In all parts of the system, including alveoli	Stretch when breathing in; recoil when breathing out, helping to force air out of the lungs
Squamous epithelium	Alveoli and blood capillaries	Thin to give a short diffusion pathway for gaseous exchange; provide a large surface area
Capillaries	In all parts of the system — many around alveoli	Provide large surface area for exchange between blood and alveolar air

Table 5 Components of the gaseous exchange system and their functions

Focus on practical skills: microscope drawings of animal tissues

During your course, you may be asked to make annotated drawings of animal tissues, such as lung and/or trachea. You should therefore study microscope slides of these two organs and be able to recognise their tissues and cells, such as the ciliated epithelia, goblet cells, smooth muscle and cartilage. You should be able to make *outline* drawings of:

- the trachea, to show distribution of the tissues
- the lungs, to show the bronchioles, branches of the pulmonary artery and vein, and the alveoli

When making these outline drawings, you should not draw any cells (as explained on p. 34). You may be asked to make some drawings, with the high power of your microscope, of a few cells from areas such as the lining of the airways (trachea, bronchus and bronchioles). You should always be able to identify the different cell types and describe their appearance, e.g. the colours that they are stained.

Key facts you must know

Gaseous exchange in the alveolus

Alveoli are tiny air-filled sacs, adapted for the efficient exchange of gases by diffusion between the air and blood capillaries. There are two main ways in which alveoli are adapted for efficiency.

Short diffusion distance

Cells lining alveoli and blood capillaries are thin, squamous epithelial cells. This allows easy diffusion of oxygen and carbon dioxide even though there are five cell membranes between the air and the haemoglobin inside red blood cells (see Figure 20).

Steep concentration gradient

Breathing ventilates the alveoli, maintaining a high concentration of oxygen in alveolar air; blood flows through capillaries in the lungs, bringing a constant supply of deoxygenated blood. The difference between the concentrations of oxygen in the air and in the blood is called a concentration gradient. Breathing and the flow of blood maintain a large difference (a steep concentration gradient), so that diffusion of oxygen from the air into the blood is rapid. Exactly the opposite happens with carbon dioxide, although the concentration gradient is not as steep.

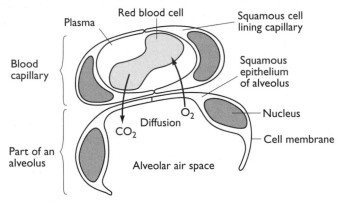

Figure 20 Features of the gaseous exchange surface in the lungs

The lungs are ventilated by movements of the diaphragm and rib cage. Humans can take shallow breaths by movement of the diaphragm alone. To breathe deeply you must use *both* the diaphragm and the ribcage. Contraction of the external intercostal muscles that run between the ribs moves the ribcage upwards and outwards during inhalation. Contraction of the internal intercostal muscles moves the ribcage downwards and inwards, which happens during forced exhalation during or after exercise, or when breathing hard.

Breathing in (inspiration/inhalation)
- Diaphragm muscles contract and pull the diaphragm down into the abdomen.
- External intercostal muscles contract and raise the ribcage.
- The volume of the thorax (chest cavity) *increases.*

- The pressure of air inside the lungs *decreases*.
- Air moves from the atmosphere to the lungs because the pressure in the atmosphere is *greater* than the air pressure in the lungs.

Breathing out (expiration/exhalation)
- Diaphragm muscles relax and the contents of the abdomen push the diaphragm upwards into the thorax.
- The ribs fall under gravity and the internal intercostal muscles may contract to lower the ribcage.
- The volume of the thorax *decreases*.
- The pressure of air in the lungs is *greater* than the pressure of air in the atmosphere, so air is forced out.

Lung volumes
Tidal volume is the volume of air that you breathe in and then breathe out during one breath. At rest it is usually about 500 cm^3. It increases when you exercise, sing or play a wind instrument.

Vital capacity is the volume of air you can force out after taking a deep breath. In young adult males it may be about 4.6 dm^3; in females, 3.1 dm^3. Athletes, singers and wind instrument players often have larger vital capacities.

These are two measurements of lung function. The **total lung volume** is the vital capacity plus the volume of air left in the lungs after you breathe out forcibly. This residual volume is usually about 1 dm^3. The total lung volume of young males may therefore be between 5 dm^3 and 6 dm^3.

Spirometer
Measurements of lung volumes such as tidal volume and vital capacity can be made with a spirometer. Figure 21 shows a typical spirometer.

A pen fixed to the lid of the spirometer makes a trace on the paper fixed to the revolving drum. As the person breathes in, the lid falls and the pen makes a downward movement. As the person breathes out, the lid rises and the pen makes an upward movement.

In Figure 22, the arrow indicates when the person starts breathing from the spirometer. We can learn the following information from the spirometer trace shown in this figure.
- Tidal volume is the difference between peak and trough. Here, it is 0.5 dm^3 (500 cm^3).
- Vital capacity is the total volume of air breathed out after taking a deep breath. Here it is 5 dm^3 (5000 cm^3).
- Breathing rate is the number of peaks or troughs per minute. Here it is 6 in 30 seconds, which is 12 breaths min^{-1}.
- Oxygen consumption is the gradient of the trace. Here it is 125 cm^3 in 30 seconds (250 cm^3 min^{-1}).

You can see more spirometer traces in Question 4 on p. 83.

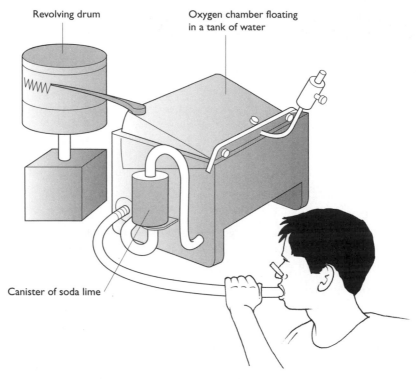

Figure 21 A spirometer

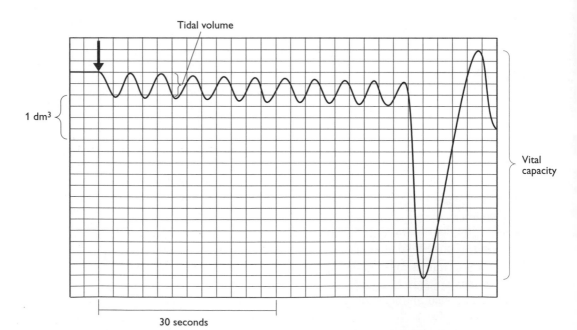

Figure 22 Measurements that can be made from a spirometer trace

Transport in animals

Key facts you must know

Substances such as oxygen, carbon dioxide and absorbed food have to be moved around the body. In unicellular organisms, such as *Amoeba*, substances can pass by diffusion or be carried in cytoplasm as it flows within the organism. Diffusion does not work in a large organism because distances are too great, and oxygen cannot be supplied fast enough from the lungs to cells elsewhere in the body; a transport system is needed. In this unit you study three systems — blood, xylem and phloem. All three are examples of **mass flow** — the movement of a fluid through a system of tubes in one direction. Table 6 compares the transport mechanisms in flowering plants and mammals.

Feature	Mammals	Flowering plants
Transport system	Circulatory system: heart + blood vessels + blood	Xylem and phloem
Gas exchange surface	Alveoli in the lungs	All cell surfaces that are in contact with the air, e.g. palisade and spongy mesophyll cells in leaves
Transport of oxygen	Oxygen in combination with haemoglobin	Oxygen and carbon dioxide diffuse through air spaces between cells
Transport of carbon dioxide	Carbon dioxide in blood plasma as HCO_3^- and in combination with haemoglobin	
Transport of carbohydrate	Glucose in solution in blood plasma	Sucrose in solution in phloem sap
Transport of water	Most of the blood plasma is water	In the xylem sap
Force to move fluids	Heart	Xylem — transpiration pull; phloem — active pumping of sugars into the phloem and hydrostatic pressure

Table 6 Comparing transport systems in mammals and flowering plants

Animals are multicellular: their bodies are made of many cells. Some small animals rely on diffusion alone to transfer oxygen, carbon dioxide, small molecules absorbed after digestion, and waste substances around the body. For example, flatworms have a large surface area to volume ratio because they are flat. Although they vary in length from less than a millimetre to over 20 metres, they are all flat. They do not have a circulatory system and their cells receive oxygen by diffusion through the body surface.

Types of circulatory system

Some animals, such as insects, have open circulatory systems; others, such as vertebrates, have closed systems. There are some blood vessels in an open circulatory system, but the blood flows out of these to bathe the tissues directly, rather than travelling in arteries, capillaries and veins. Vertebrates, such as fish and mammals, have closed circulations in which the blood flows through the body confined within blood vessels. Substances are exchanged between blood and tissues across the walls of capillaries — the tiniest blood vessels.

Key concepts you must understand

Closed circulations have three important components:

- the blood — red blood cells, white blood cells, platelets and plasma
- blood vessels — arteries, arterioles, capillaries, venules and veins
- the heart — the pump for circulating blood through the vessels

Figure 23 shows simple views of fish and mammalian circulatory systems. Fish have a single circulation: the blood passes from the heart to the gills and then immediately

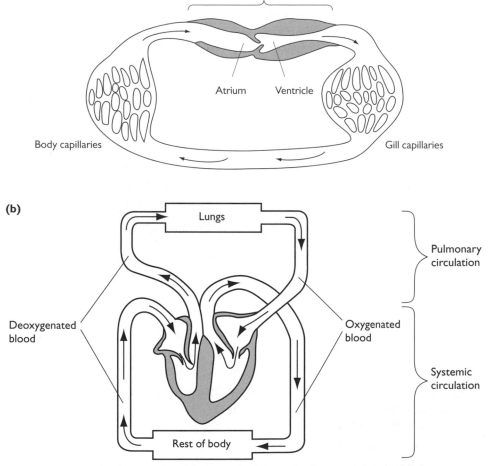

***Figure 23** (a) The fish circulatory system. Follow the pathway from the gills and back to see why it is called a single circulation. (b) The mammalian circulatory system. Follow the pathway from the lungs and back to see why it is called a double circulation.*

to the rest of the body. Blood passes through the heart once during a complete circulation of the body. Mammals have a double circulation in which the blood passes through the heart twice in one complete circulation of the body. The circuit from the heart to the lungs and back is the **pulmonary circulation**. The circuit from the heart to the rest of the body and back is the **systemic circulation**.

The mammalian heart

Key facts you must know

The heart is a muscular pump. It is made of cardiac muscle and is described as myogenic (it stimulates itself to beat). You should be familiar with the following features of the heart:

- There are four chambers — two atria and two ventricles.
- There are two pumps working in series — the right side of the heart pumps deoxygenated blood to the lungs in the **pulmonary circulation**; the left side pumps oxygenated blood to the rest of the body through the **systemic circulation**.
- The left and right atria have thin walls because they pump blood into the ventricles, which are only a short distance from the atria.
- The left and right ventricles have thick walls because they pump blood a greater distance and against a greater resistance than the atria.
- There are valves in the heart to prevent backflow and to ensure the blood follows the correct pathway.
- The volume of blood ejected by each chamber is the same during one beat, but the volume can change from beat to beat in response to the body's demand for oxygen.

Stroke volume is the volume of blood ejected from each ventricle during one beat. At rest it may be about 150 cm^3. **Cardiac output** is the volume of blood ejected from each of the ventricles during 1 minute:

cardiac output = stroke volume × heart rate

At rest it may be about $150 \times 70 = 10\,500$ cm^3 = 10.5 dm^3 per minute.

The **cardiac cycle** describes the sequence of changes that occurs in the heart during one heart beat.

Drawings and diagrams of the heart usually show it viewed from the front of the body. Figure 24 shows the external structure of the heart with the major blood vessels. Note the **coronary arteries** that supply the heart muscle with oxygenated blood. They branch from the base of the aorta. Figure 25 shows the internal structure of the heart.

Table 7 shows the functions of the chambers of the adult human heart. The ventricles are thicker than the atria because they generate greater pressures. The left ventricle is thicker than the right ventricle because it has to pump blood into the

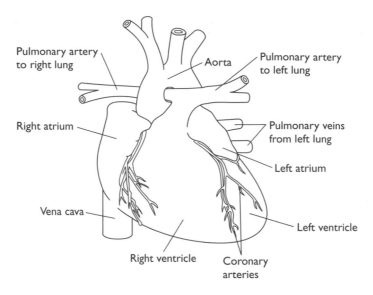

Figure 24 An external view of the heart

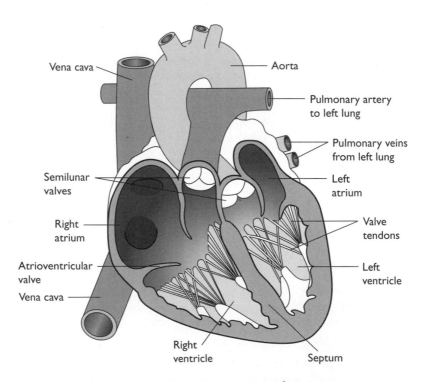

Figure 25 A vertical section through the heart

Chamber of the heart	Receives blood from...	Pumps blood to...
Right atrium	...the body through the vena cava	...the right ventricle
Right ventricle	...the right atrium	...the lungs through the pulmonary artery
Left atrium	...the lungs through the pulmonary veins	...the left ventricle
Left ventricle	...the left atrium	...the body through the aorta

Table 7 The functions of the four chambers of the mammalian heart

systemic circulation that has arteries in parallel. A high pressure is needed to ensure that all the organs receive a good supply of blood, even if the flow to some areas increases significantly. For example, when much more blood flows to the muscles during exercise than when at rest, the blood supply to organs such as the brain and the kidneys must still be maintained.

The pulmonary circulation provides a lesser resistance to flow than the systemic circulation. The lungs are a spongy tissue and blood fills most of the capillaries in the lungs. A low blood pressure in the pulmonary circulation ensures that fluid does not leak out of the pulmonary capillaries, causing fluid to accumulate in the alveoli. This fluid accumulation may occur in people who have severe emphysema, where the right ventricle generates a higher blood pressure than normal.

Control of the heart

The heart beat is controlled by the sino-atrial node (SAN) in the right atrium. The SAN is a special region of muscle cells that emits electrical pulses similar to those that pass along nerve cells. These travel across the muscle in the atria and cause them to contract together. The electrical impulses are prevented from reaching the ventricle muscles directly by a ring of fibrous tissue between the atria and the ventricles. The atrioventricular node (AVN) is in the central septum at the junction between the atria and ventricles. The AVN delays the impulses so that they reach the ventricles after these chambers have filled with blood from the atria. Impulses are relayed by the AVN along Purkyne tissue, which conducts to muscles at the base of the ventricles so that this area contracts first. This forces blood from the bottom of the ventricles upwards into the arteries. As this happens, the rest of the ventricle muscles contract so that the ventricles empty completely.

Nerves that supply the heart alter the rate of contraction. They do not stimulate the heart to beat each time.

The cardiac cycle

The spread of impulses from the SAN starts a series of changes that comprise the cardiac cycle. Imagine that the individual drawings in Figure 26 are still pictures from a film of the heart beating. The small arrows in the heart show where the blood is flowing at each stage. Figure 27 shows the changes in blood pressure in the left atrium, left ventricle and the aorta. The blood pressure is recorded by placing pressure sensors in each of these three places.

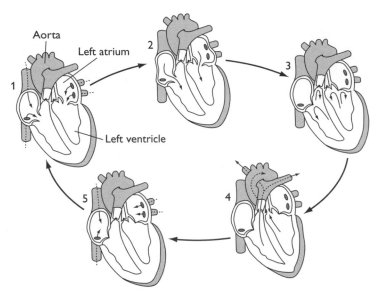

Figure 26 The cardiac cycle

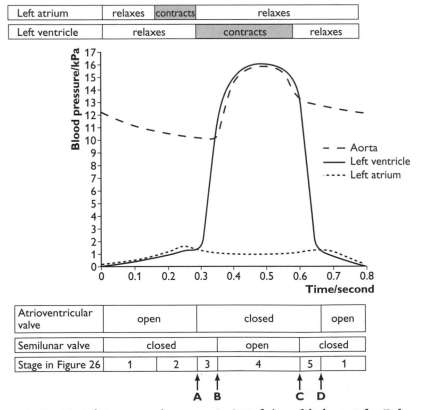

Left atrium	relaxes	contracts	relaxes	

Left ventricle	relaxes		contracts	relaxes

Atrioventricular valve	open		closed		open
Semilunar valve	closed		open		closed
Stage in Figure 26	1	2	3	4	5	1

Figure 27 Contraction occurs in stages 2, 3 and 4 — this is systole. Relaxation occurs in stages 5 and 1 — this is diastole.

Notice the following:

- The blood pressure in the atria and the ventricles falls near to 0 kPa during each cycle because there are times when there is little blood in these chambers.
- The pressure in the aorta does not fall below about 10 kPa. Its wall stretches as blood surges into it from the left ventricle, and then recoils to maintain the blood pressure and to keep blood flowing.
- When the pressure in the left ventricle is greater than that in the left atrium, the atrioventricular valve closes to stop blood flowing back into the atrium. The tendons at the base of the valve stop the blood 'blowing back' into the atrium. This occurs at point A in Figure 27.
- When the pressure in the ventricle is greater than that in the aorta, the semilunar valve opens and the blood flows from the ventricle to the aorta. This occurs at point B in Figure 27.
- When the pressure in the aorta is greater than that in the ventricle, the semilunar valve fills with blood, closes off the aorta and prevents backflow. This occurs at point C in Figure 27.
- When the pressure in the left atrium is greater than the pressure in the left ventricle, the atrioventricular valve opens and blood flows from the left atrium into the ventricle. This occurs at point D in Figure 27.

Now, position a ruler on Figure 27 over the vertical axis at time 0.

- Move the ruler across the graph to the right and follow the changes to the blood pressure in the ventricle. Look at the stages (1–5) in Figure 26 to follow the changes to the left ventricle. Move the ruler back to 0 and repeat the procedure, this time following the changes in the left atrium, and then again for the changes in the aorta.
- Think about the opening and closing of the semilunar and atrioventricular valves. Look at the blood pressure either side of points A, B, C and D in Figure 27 and at Figure 26 to check whether these valves are opening or closing at each point in the cycle.
- It takes 0.8 seconds to complete this cardiac cycle. This means that there are 60/0.8 = 75 beats per minute.

For further information, look at the animation of the cardiac cycle at:
  http://library.med.utah.edu/kw/pharm/hyper_heart1.html

You can expect to be asked about the cardiac cycle graph, so it is well worth studying Figures 26 and 27 in some detail.

Electrocardiograms

One way to check on the health of the heart is to record its electrical activity by using electrocardiography. Electrodes are attached to the body to give an electrocardiogram (ECG). Figure 28 shows a normal ECG trace. There are some abnormal ECG traces in Question 5 on p. 87.

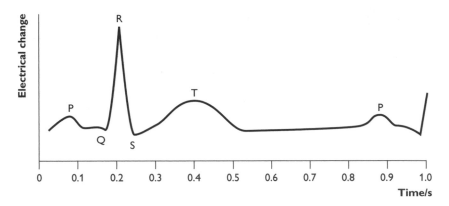

Figure 28 A normal ECG trace

Links   You may carry out a heart dissection as the qualitative task in Unit F213. If you are asked to make annotated drawings of your dissection, do not expect the interior of the heart to look like the diagrams you see in books. Use these diagrams to anticipate what to expect, but draw what you see. You may be asked to measure the thickness of the walls of the four chambers and record them on your drawing, and explain the differences in thickness.

Blood vessels

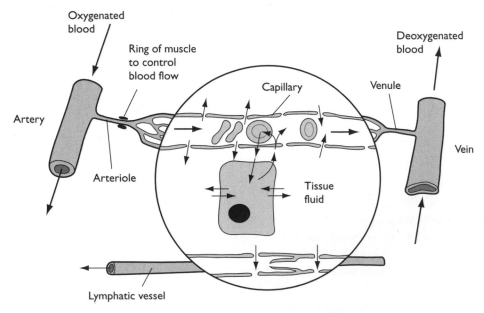

Figure 29 Blood flow through a capillary bed

Key concepts you must understand

An important function of the blood is to transport gases (oxygen and carbon dioxide), nutrients, hormones and waste products, such as urea. During each circuit of the body, blood flows through capillaries in the lungs and other organs, such as the stomach, liver and kidneys. Figure 29 shows the path taken by blood as it flows through a capillary bed in an organ. Capillaries are the **exchange vessels** of the circulatory system, where substances pass into and out of the blood.

Blood is supplied to an organ by an artery. It then flows through arterioles and then capillaries where exchanges occur between blood and tissue fluid. Blood drains through venules and then veins to return to the heart. Capillaries are very small, which is why the central area in Figure 29 is shown magnified.

Key facts you must know

Figure 30 shows cross-sections of an artery and a vein. Table 8 compares the structure and functions of arteries and veins.

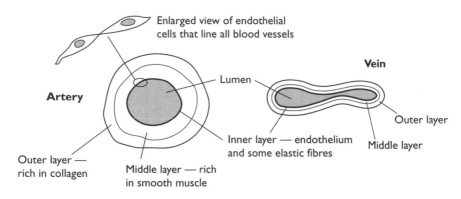

Figure 30 Cross-sections of an artery and a vein

Feature	Artery	Vein
Width of wall	Thick	Thin
Components of wall	Lined by endothelium; rest of wall contains smooth muscle, elastic fibres, collagen	As artery, but less smooth muscle, elastic tissue and collagen
Semilunar valves	No	Yes, to prevent backflow
Blood pressure	High	Low
Direction of blood flow	Heart to organs and tissues	Organs and tissues to heart
Function	Elastic fibres recoil to maintain high pressure in arteries to overcome resistance of the circulation system	Return blood to the heart — assisted by squeezing action of surrounding muscles which help to push blood towards heart

Table 8 The structure and functions of arteries and veins

As blood flows around the body, its pressure changes. Blood pressure is necessary — without it the blood would not flow through the blood vessels. The vessels present a resistance to blood flow and the contraction of the heart raises the pressure of the blood, forcing it through the circulation. There is a high pressure in the arteries so that blood is delivered efficiently to organs. Blood then flows through many smaller blood vessels — arterioles — before flowing through an even larger number of capillaries. As the diameter of the vessels decreases, the resistance to flow increases significantly.

Arterioles are surrounded by smooth muscle which can contract to reduce the size of the lumen, so that blood flow to the capillaries decreases. This allows blood to be diverted elsewhere, for example from skin and gut to muscles during exercise. There is only enough blood to fill 25% of the capillaries at any one time, so arterioles play an important function in controlling the flow of blood to tissues, rather like taps controlling the flow of water. Arteries and veins may be metres in length (think of a blue whale or a giraffe); arterioles, capillaries and venules are only a few millimetres in length. Changes in blood pressure in the systemic circuit are shown in Figure 31.

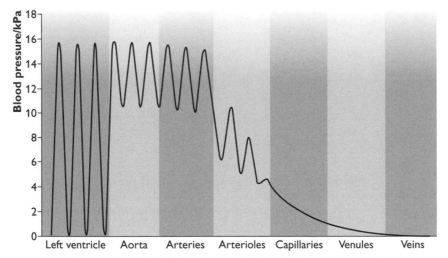

Figure 31 The changes in blood pressure at different places in the systemic circulation (not drawn to scale).

The graph in Figure 31 shows the pressure changes in three successive heart beats and the effect of these in the arteries and other vessels. Notice that there are three peaks and troughs in the left ventricle, which are repeated in the aorta and the arteries. The rise and fall in blood pressure is greatest in the left ventricle. This is then reduced in the aorta and main arteries and becomes much smaller in the arterioles and capillaries, where the blood pressure decreases considerably. Blood pressure is lowest in the venules and veins. From Figure 31 you can see why arteries have thick, muscular and elastic walls (to withstand high blood pressure), arterioles have muscular walls (to damp down blood pressure) and veins have thin walls (as the blood has a low pressure). Capillaries have thin walls because they are **exchange vessels** (see Figures 32 and 33).

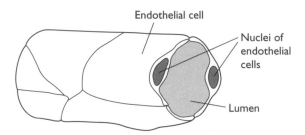

Figure 32 A capillary lined by endothelial cells

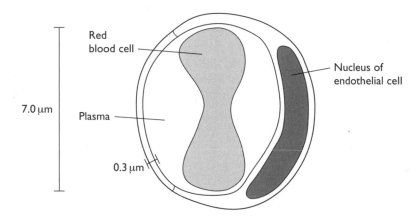

Figure 33 Cross-section of a capillary. Notice that red blood cells just fit inside the vessel and that the endothelial cells are thin to help the exchange of substances with the blood.

Exchanges that occur as blood flows through capillaries include:
- oxygen diffusing out of the blood into tissue fluid
- carbon dioxide diffusing from tissue fluid into the blood
- water and dissolved substances, such as glucose and amino acids, being forced out by the pressure of the blood

Water and substances that are forced out by high pressure are **filtered** from the blood. As blood flows through the capillaries its pressure decreases, which makes it possible for water to drain back into the blood plasma by osmosis. This is because the blood contains solutes, such as albumen, which give the blood plasma a lower water potential than the tissue fluid. Albumen is a large protein molecule that rarely leaves the blood.

Feature	Blood	Tissue fluid	Lymph
Where found	In blood vessels	Surrounding cells	In lymphatic vessels
Components:			
● red blood cells	✓	✗	✗
● white blood cells	✓	✓ (some)	✓ (some)
● fats	✓ (as lipoproteins)	✓	✓ (especially after a meal)
● glucose	✓	✓	very little
● proteins	✓	✓ (some)	✓ (some, e.g. antibodies)
Functions	Transport	Bathes cells — all exchanges between blood and cells occur through tissue fluid	Drains excess tissue fluid, preventing a build up leading to oedema

Table 9 The composition and functions of three body fluids

Not all the tissue fluid is drained this way. Within the tissues are small, blind-ended tubes called lymphatic vessels, which act as a 'drainage system'. Tissue fluid flows into the lymphatic vessels and then flows slowly towards large lymphatic vessels that empty into the blood near the heart. The fluid inside lymphatic vessels is called lymph, and is similar in composition to tissue fluid. At intervals along the lymphatic vessels are lymph nodes. These contain lymphocytes, some of which flow into the blood via the lymph. Lymph also drains fat from the small intestine so that after a meal it often appears as a white suspension.

Blood cells

You should be able to recognise the types of blood cell shown in Figure 34, both in photographs and through the microscope.

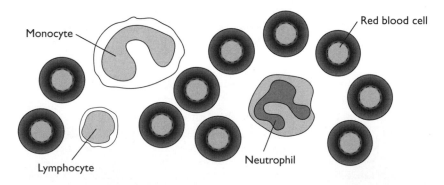

Figure 34 A drawing of a blood smear, as seen through a light microscope

Table 10 compares the structures of the main types of blood cell. Neutrophils are the most common type of phagocyte in the blood: comprising approximately 70% of all white blood cells. Monocytes are transported in the blood from the bone marrow, where they are produced, to tissues, such as lymph nodes, where they become macrophages — another type of phagocytic cell.

Feature	Red blood cells (erythrocytes)	Neutrophils	Lymphocytes
Diameter/μm	7	9	4–6
Nucleus	✗ (lost during development in bone marrow)	✓ (lobed)	✓ (large — fills most of the cell)
Organelles	None — cytoplasm is full of haemoglobin molecules	Present, e.g. mitochondria; lysosomes containing enzymes to break down bacteria and other pathogens	Present — especially rough endoplasmic reticulum and Golgi apparatus in activated B cells (also known as plasma cells)

Table 10 Structure of three types of blood cell

Links You need to know about two types of lymphocyte in Module 2 of Unit F212. These are B and T lymphocytes, which have different functions during an immune response. Activated B lymphocytes divide to become plasma cells, which secrete antibody molecules. Plasma cells are full of rough endoplasmic reticulum for the production of protein and have a Golgi apparatus for the packaging and release of antibody molecules. Remember that antibodies are made of protein. T-helper cells stimulate B lymphocytes to divide and T-killer cells search out and kill cells that are infected with viruses.

Key facts you must know

Cells respire. To respire aerobically they need a supply of oxygen and a way for waste carbon dioxide to be removed. Blood is adapted to achieve this transport. If we only had a watery fluid to transport oxygen and carbon dioxide, we would not be able to carry these gases efficiently. Oxygen is not very soluble in water. The volume of oxygen that will dissolve in water is about 0.3 cm^3 per 100 cm^3. Blood can carry 20 cm^3 of oxygen per 100 cm^3. Carbon dioxide is much more soluble in water than oxygen is, and about 2.6 cm^3 per 100 cm^3 could be transported in solution. However, blood can carry 50–60 cm^3 of carbon dioxide per 100 cm^3. How is this possible?

Haemoglobin (Hb) transports almost all the oxygen in the blood and some of the carbon dioxide. Each red blood cell has about 280 million molecules of haemoglobin. You should consider the structure of haemoglobin, which you study in Module 1 of Unit F212. You can also find information about the structure of haemoglobin at:

http://www.3dchem.com/molecules.asp?ID=213#

Haemoglobin is a protein composed of four sub-units, each one containing a haem group, which binds oxygen. Each haem binds one molecule of oxygen (O_2), so each haemoglobin molecule can bind to four molecules of oxygen ($4O_2$) to form oxyhaemoglobin:

$$Hb \qquad + \quad 4O_2 \qquad\qquad\qquad \rightleftharpoons \quad HbO_8$$

haemoglobin + 4 molecules of oxygen $\rightleftharpoons$ oxyhaemoglobin

When carbon dioxide dissolves in water, much of it reacts to form carbonic acid, which dissociates (breaks up) to form hydrogen ions and hydrogencarbonate ions:

$$CO_2 \quad + \quad H_2O \quad \rightleftharpoons \quad H_2CO_3 \quad \rightleftharpoons \quad H^+ \quad + \quad HCO_3^-$$

| carbon dioxide | + | water | $\rightleftharpoons$ | carbonic acid | $\rightleftharpoons$ | hydrogen ions | + | hydrogencarbonate ions |

Blood can carry much more carbon dioxide than water can because there is a fast-acting enzyme inside red blood cells. This enzyme is **carbonic anhydrase**. It catalyses the formation of carbonic acid, which immediately dissociates to form hydrogen ions and hydrogencarbonate ions. Large quantities of hydrogencarbonate ions are carried in the blood plasma in association with sodium ions. Some carbon dioxide also attaches to the $-NH_2$ groups (amino groups) at the end of the polypeptides in haemoglobin to form carbamino-haemoglobin, and some remains in solution (as carbon dioxide) in the plasma.

Transport of oxygen

Key concepts you must understand

In the lungs, deoxygenated blood flows very close to alveolar air. The air in the alveoli is rich in oxygen. This richness is expressed as its partial pressure (abbreviated to pO_2), which is the part of the air pressure that oxygen exerts. Approximately 13–14% of the air inside the alveoli is oxygen. The total air pressure is about 100 kPa, so the partial pressure of oxygen in the alveoli is close to 13–14 kPa (see p. 11 if you are unsure about pressure units). Deoxygenated blood flowing into the lungs has a low concentration of oxygen. Alveolar air is rich in oxygen, so a concentration gradient exists between the air and the blood, and oxygen diffuses from the air in the alveoli into the blood.

The oxygenated blood leaving the lungs carries almost the full amount of oxygen it can possibly carry. Tissues such as muscle tissues and those in the gut, liver and kidney use oxygen in respiration. The concentration of oxygen in these tissues is low, equivalent to a partial pressure of approximately 5.0 kPa. This means that oxygen diffuses from the blood into the tissues down a concentration gradient. Blood loses about 30% of the oxygen it carries as it flows through the tissues when you are at rest (not doing any exercise).

To find out how much oxygen is transported by haemoglobin, small samples of blood are exposed to gas mixtures with different concentrations of oxygen. The volume of oxygen absorbed by the haemoglobin in each sample of blood is determined and expressed as a percentage of the maximum volume that haemoglobin absorbs. The results are shown as an oxygen haemoglobin dissociation curve (see Figure 35). The concentration of oxygen is shown as the partial pressure of oxygen in the gas mixture.

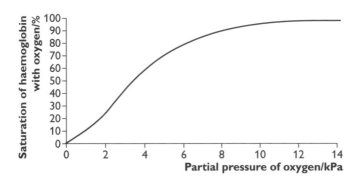

Figure 35 The results of an investigation into the effects of different air mixtures on the saturation of haemoglobin with oxygen

The line of best fit drawn on the graph is known as the oxygen haemoglobin dissociation curve. The sigmoid shape (or S shape) of the line is important. Remember that the graph shows the results of an experiment on blood carried out in the laboratory. How does this relate to the actual situation in the mammalian body? If we take some figures from the graph, we should be able to see how to use this information. Table 11 shows the saturation of haemoglobin with oxygen at different partial pressures. The partial pressures chosen correspond with those in different parts of the circulation.

Site in the body	Partial pressure of oxygen/kPa	Saturation of haemoglobin with oxygen/%
Lungs	13.0	98
Tissues, including muscles at rest	5.0	70
Muscles during strenuous exercise	3.0	43
Muscles at exhaustion	2.0	20
Placenta	4.0	60

Table 11

We can see from Figure 35 and Table 11 that haemoglobin is:
- nearly fully saturated at the partial pressure of oxygen in the lungs
- about 70% saturated at the partial pressure in the tissues
- about 45% saturated in areas with very low partial pressures of oxygen, such as actively respiring muscle

As blood flows through capillaries, oxyhaemoglobin releases oxygen *in response to the low concentration of oxygen in the tissues*. Haemoglobin has a high affinity for oxygen at high partial pressures and a low affinity at low partial pressures.

Gaseous exchange between maternal blood and fetal blood occurs across the placenta. In order to be nearly fully saturated with oxygen, fetal haemoglobin must have a higher affinity for oxygen than adult haemoglobin. When experimenters investigated fetal blood using the same method as used to give the results shown in Figure 35, they found when they plotted the dissociation curve that it was *to the left* of the curve for adult haemoglobin. The partial pressure of oxygen at the placenta is about 4.0 kPa. At this partial pressure, adult blood is close to 60% saturated, which means that oxyhaemoglobin gives up its oxygen to the surrounding tissues in the placenta. Fetal haemoglobin is about 80% saturated at this partial pressure, so it absorbs much of the oxygen released by the mother's blood. Tissues in the placenta absorb the rest.

Transport of carbon dioxide

Figure 36 shows the events that occur as carbon dioxide diffuses into the blood in tissues.

When the changes shown in Figure 36 occur, hydrogen ions (H^+) are released. These would reduce the pH of blood cells if left unchecked, so haemoglobin binds the hydrogen ions to become haemoglobinic acid (HHb). This prevents a decrease in pH. Haemoglobin therefore acts as a **buffer** to the change in pH, stopping it from decreasing.

When the blood reaches the lungs, these changes go into reverse, as shown in Figure 37.

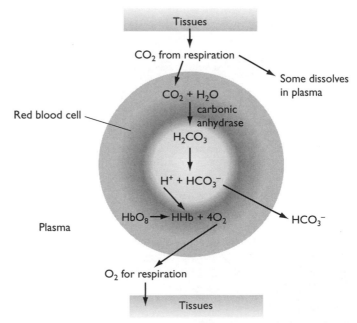

Figure 36 Most of the carbon dioxide diffuses into red blood cells and is converted to hydrogencarbonate ions by the action of carbonic anhydrase. Some carbon dioxide dissolves in the plasma.

content guidance

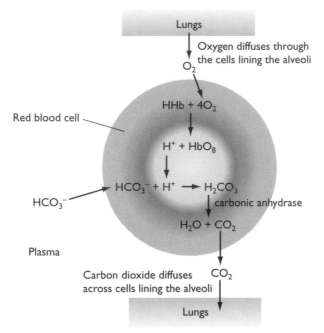

Figure 37 These events occur as blood flows through capillaries in the alveoli, so that carbon dioxide diffuses into alveolar air

The Bohr effect

When carbon dioxide diffuses into the blood, it stimulates haemoglobin to release even more oxygen than it would if it only responded to the low concentration of oxygen. This can be explained by the fact that when haemoglobin accepts hydrogen ions to become haemoglobinic acid (HHb), it stimulates the molecule to give up oxygen (see Figure 36). When the experiment with gas mixtures was repeated using carbon dioxide as well, it was discovered that carbon dioxide *decreased* the affinity of haemoglobin for oxygen. Figure 38 shows the effect when the results are plotted on a graph.

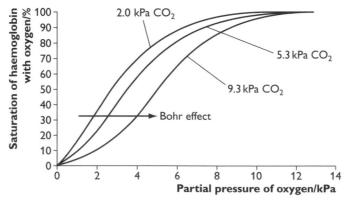

Figure 38 The Bohr effect. When carbon dioxide was added to the gas mixtures, haemoglobin became less saturated with oxygen.

This shift of the curve to the right is known as the Bohr effect, after the Danish scientist who discovered it. The best way to understand the Bohr effect is to take some figures from the graph. Table 12 shows the effect of increasing the partial pressure of carbon dioxide on the saturation of haemoglobin. The figures are taken for the *same* partial pressure of oxygen (pO_2 = 3.0 kPa, which corresponds with that in the tissues when they are respiring actively). Notice that the haemoglobin is much less saturated with oxygen when the pCO_2 is 9.3 kPa. As blood flows through the capillaries it gives up more oxygen than it would have done if there were less carbon dioxide present.

Partial pressure of carbon dioxide/kPa	% saturation of haemoglobin with oxygen at pO_2 of 3.0 kPa
2.0	55
5.3	40
9.3	20

Table 12

Links If fetal haemoglobin has a higher affinity for oxygen than adult haemoglobin, why don't we keep it throughout life? Unfortunately, because it has a higher affinity, it does not release its oxygen so well in respiring tissues. After birth, tissues need a much greater supply of oxygen, which is provided by adult haemoglobin — a switch occurs during the first few years of life. Sometimes this switch does not happen, resulting in the tissues being starved of oxygen. This is what happens in people who have thalassaemia, a genetic disease that occurs most frequently in people from countries around the Mediterranean. Thalassaemia originated as a mutation in one of the genes that codes for haemoglobin. You will learn more about how genes code for proteins in Unit F212, and more about mutation in the A2 Unit F215.

Red blood cells are unusual because they have no membrane-bound organelles, such as mitochondria and endoplasmic reticulum, and no nucleus. Does this make them prokaryotes? Certainly not! As red cells develop in bone marrow, they lose their nuclei, resulting in a biconcave shape with a large surface area to volume ratio (see p. 38). They are eukaryotic cells.

In the qualitative task in Unit F213, you may be given a microscope slide or a photomicrograph of a blood smear and be expected to draw the different types of blood cell. Make sure you have seen some of these and some good photographs, so that you can recognise the cells. Red blood cells are easy, but it takes a while to see the difference between lymphocytes and neutrophils. Look carefully for the lobed nucleus of the neutrophil — see Figure 34. You also need to recognise arteries and veins in photographs and microscope slides and be able to draw them under the microscope.

Transport in plants

Key concepts you must understand

Flowering plants need transport systems to move water and assimilates, such as sucrose and amino acids. Assimilates are so called because they have been made from simple substances, such as water, carbon dioxide and ions (e.g. nitrate ions), which have been taken from the environment and converted into compounds that are incorporated into the plant. Water is absorbed by roots and is required by stems, leaves, flowers and fruits. Sugars are made by leaves but are required by roots, storage organs (such as potato tubers), flowers, fruits and seeds. The parts of the plants where water and assimilates are loaded into the transport systems are called **sources**. The parts where they are unloaded are called **sinks**. Transport systems are needed because the distances between sources and sinks are large — even in a small weed the distance is too great for the movement to occur rapidly enough by diffusion. These distances are even more substantial in tall trees such as giant redwoods, which grow up to 80 metres in height.

There are two transport systems in plants:
- **xylem** for water and mineral ions
- **phloem** for assimilates, such as sucrose and amino acids

The contents of xylem and phloem move by mass flow. Everything within each 'tube' in these tissues moves in the same direction at the same time.

The movement of water in the xylem depends on transpiration, which is the evaporation of water from the leaves and other aerial parts of plants. The source of energy that drives transpiration comes from the sun. The plant provides a system of channels for water to flow, but does not provide energy for the movement of water in the xylem. There are many damp surfaces inside leaves from which evaporation occurs, because each cell has its own surface for gaseous exchange. The consequence is that the air spaces are fully saturated with water vapour. As soon as stomata open to allow carbon dioxide to diffuse into the leaf, water vapour diffuses out. This is why transpiration is an inevitable consequence of the very large surface area for gaseous exchange inside leaves.

Movement in the phloem is by translocation. Literally, translocation means 'from place to place', but it is the name given to the mass flow of assimilates dissolved in water that occurs in phloem tissue. This is driven by energy from the plant.

Key facts you must know

Figure 39 shows cross-sections of a leaf, a root and a stem of a typical flowering plant. You should be able to show on such diagrams where the xylem and phloem are situated. Figure 40 is a photograph of the central area of a root, as seen through the medium power of a microscope. You should be able to identify the tissues labelled here.

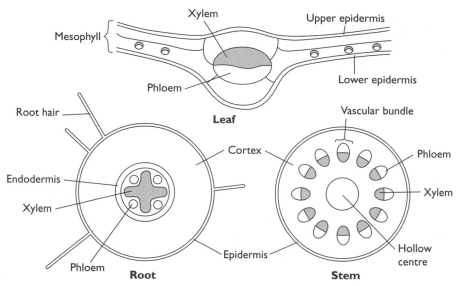

Figure 39 The distribution of xylem and phloem in cross-sections of leaf, root and stem

Xylem tissue consists of:

- vessel elements — dead, empty cells arranged into continuous columns called vessels
- parenchyma cells — living cells found between the vessels

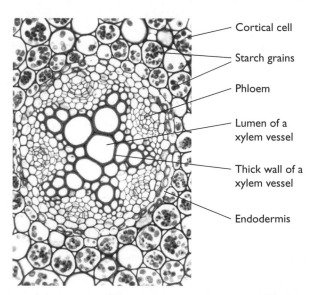

Figure 40 This photograph shows what you should be able to see under the medium power of a microscope when you look at the centre of a cross-section of a root. Notice that the xylem in this case is in the form of a five-pointed star.

Figure 41 shows details of xylem vessels and how they are adapted to transport water and provide support.

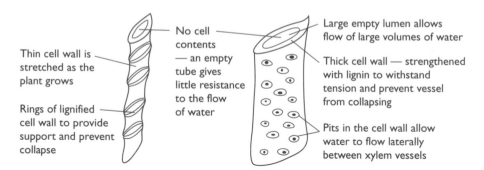

Thin cell wall is stretched as the plant grows

No cell contents — an empty tube gives little resistance to the flow of water

Rings of lignified cell wall to provide support and prevent collapse

Large empty lumen allows flow of large volumes of water

Thick cell wall — strengthened with lignin to withstand tension and prevent vessel from collapsing

Pits in the cell wall allow water to flow laterally between xylem vessels

Figure 41 Two xylem vessel elements. (a) A narrow vessel thickened with rings. (b) A wider vessel with pits to allow lateral movement of water.

Phloem tissue consists of:

- phloem sieve tube elements — living cells arranged into continuous columns called sieve tubes
- companion cells — smaller, very active cells

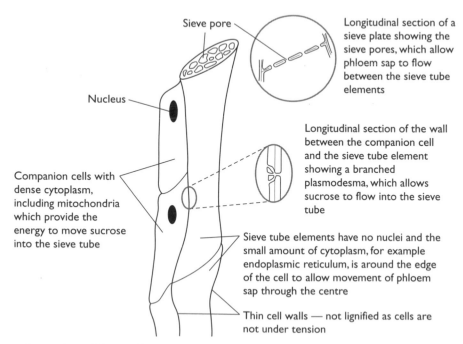

Sieve pore

Nucleus

Companion cells with dense cytoplasm, including mitochondria which provide the energy to move sucrose into the sieve tube

Longitudinal section of a sieve plate showing the sieve pores, which allow phloem sap to flow between the sieve tube elements

Longitudinal section of the wall between the companion cell and the sieve tube element showing a branched plasmodesma, which allows sucrose to flow into the sieve tube

Sieve tube elements have no nuclei and the small amount of cytoplasm, for example endoplasmic reticulum, is around the edge of the cell to allow movement of phloem sap through the centre

Thin cell walls — not lignified as cells are not under tension

Figure 42 Phloem sieve tubes and companion cells, showing how they are adapted for their functions. Plasmodesmata are small tubes of cytoplasm that pass through the cell wall. They are lined by membrane continuous with the cell surface membrane.

Transport of water in plants

We will start with two important concepts from Module 1 of this unit — osmosis and water potential (see pp. 25–26).

Figure 43 shows the movement of water between some mesophyll cells. Cell P has a higher water potential than cells Q and R. This may be because Q and R have more solutes in them than P, or because they are losing more water by evaporation to the air than P is. The arrows show the direction taken by water. The symbol Ψ is used to represent water potential. Remember that –300 kPa is *greater than* –400 kPa, so water moves from a higher water potential (P) to a lower water potential (Q). You should be able to state the direction water takes when given some water potentials, such as those in Figure 43.

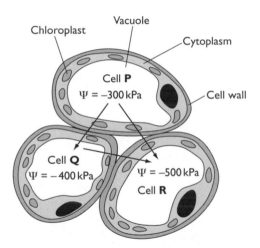

***Figure 43** The arrows show the direction of water movement between three mesophyll cells in a leaf. Cell P has the highest water potential and the water potential of cell Q is higher than that of cell R.*

Most of the water absorbed by plants is lost to the atmosphere in transpiration. Water is absorbed by root hair cells and passes across the cortex of the root, through the endodermis and into the xylem in the central region (see Figure 44). From here it travels inside xylem vessels until it reaches the leaves, where it may reach cells and:
- be used as a raw material for photosynthesis, or
- enter the vacuole to give it turgidity and help with support, or
- pass to the cell wall and evaporate into the air spaces in the leaf

Water vapour that evaporates from cell walls may diffuse through the stomata into the atmosphere outside the leaf.

As water travels across the cortex in the root and across the leaf there are two main pathways it may follow (see Figure 44):
- the **apoplast** pathway — along cell walls
- the **symplast** pathway — from cell to cell through the plasmodesmata

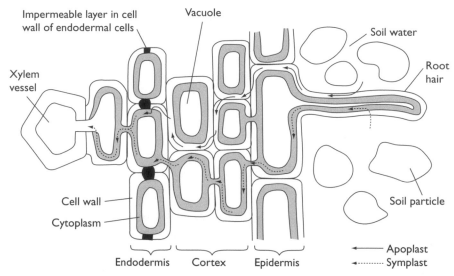

Figure 44 The arrows show the pathways taken by water as it moves from the soil, into a root hair, across the cortex, through the endodermis and into the xylem. Plasmodesmata are shown as the shaded areas passing through the cell walls, but they are not as big as shown here. Root hair cells provide a large surface area for the absorption of water.

Most of the water probably follows the pathway of least resistance, the apoplast pathway. The endodermis is a layer of cells that have impermeable material between the cell walls. This is a barrier to the apoplast pathway, so water has to travel through cells into xylem vessels. There is a water potential gradient here, so that water travels from the cortex by osmosis across the cells and into the xylem. The function of the endodermis is probably to select ions to pump from the cortex into the xylem and then transport to the rest of the plant.

The force that draws water up through xylem vessels is **transpiration pull**. Water evaporates from the cell surfaces inside the leaf. This makes the air spaces inside the leaves fully saturated with water vapour. If the stomata are open, then water vapour escapes by diffusion. Transpiration is the combined effect of evaporation from the internal surfaces of leaves and the diffusion of water vapour out of the leaves. Water moves through plants because of cohesive forces between water molecules and the adhesive forces between water and the cellulose in cell walls. This is known as cohesion-tension. Various factors influence the rate at which transpiration occurs:

- Temperature — on hot days, the rate of evaporation increases and the air holds more water. Increasing temperature tends to increase the rate of transpiration.
- Humidity — on very humid days, the atmosphere may hold as much water as the air inside the leaves. This means that there is little or no gradient for the diffusion of water vapour. Increasing humidity tends to decrease the rate of transpiration.
- Wind speed — on windy days, water vapour molecules are blown away from the leaf surface as soon as they pass through the stomata. Increasing air speed tends to increase the rate of transpiration.

● Light intensity — in most plants, stomata open during daylight hours to obtain carbon dioxide for photosynthesis. When stomata are open it is inevitable that water vapour will diffuse out of the leaf down the diffusion gradient. At night, plants cannot photosynthesise, so they close their stomata to conserve water. As light intensity increases, most plants open their stomata wider to obtain as much carbon dioxide as they can. This tends to increase the rate of transpiration.

Some desert plants open their stomata at night to take in carbon dioxide and close them during the day to conserve water.

Focus on practical skills: Measuring rates of transpiration

You can use a potometer to measure the rate at which leafy shoots cut from plants absorb water. Potometers like the one in Figure 45 measure rates of water uptake, *not* rates of transpiration. If they are put onto a balance, they can measure *both* the rate of water uptake (by following the movement of the bubble of air) *and* the rate of transpiration (by measuring the loss in mass).

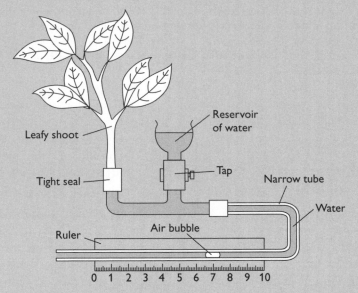

Figure 45 A typical school or college potometer for measuring the rate of water uptake by leafy shoots

You should take a number of precautions when setting up a potometer:

● The leafy shoot should be cut under water and placed into the potometer under water so that air does not enter the xylem vessels and block them.

● The leafy shoot should be left in the potometer for some time to adjust before any readings are taken.

● Conditions around the leafy shoot should remain constant while readings are taken. Repeat readings should be taken to ensure the results are reliable.

- Conditions can be changed by altering the temperature, humidity, wind speed and light intensity. While investigating one factor, such as temperature, the other factors should be kept constant. This is difficult to achieve in a school or college laboratory unless you have access to an environmental chamber that maintains constant conditions.

Readings taken from a potometer are given as distance travelled (by the air bubble) in a certain period of time. It is possible to calculate the volume of water that has been absorbed if you know the radius of the narrow tube. For a tube with a radius of 1 mm, if the bubble travels 20 mm in 15 minutes, the rate of water absorption is calculated as follows (where r = radius of narrow tube, and h = distance travelled by air bubble):

volume of a cylinder = $\pi r^2 h$ = 3.14 × 1 × 20 = 62.8 mm^3

rate of water uptake = 62.8/15 = 4.2 mm^3 min^{-1} (to the nearest 0.1 mm^3 min^{-1})

If the quantitative task involved taking measurements with a potometer, the evaluative task would involve assessing the reliability, validity and accuracy of the results.

Xerophytes

Xerophytes are plants that are adapted to living in places where there is a shortage of water. There are various adaptations to *reduce* water loss in the leaves of these plants, some of which are described in Table 13.

Feature	Adaptation for reduction of water loss
Leaf is permanently rolled or rolls up in dry conditions	Air is trapped inside the leaf; water vapour diffuses into the air, but is lost slowly to the atmosphere; the humid air is trapped and reduces the diffusion of water vapour from the stomata; leaves that do this have their stomata facing inwards when the leaf is rolled
Thick cuticle	Cuticle is made of waxy substances that waterproof the leaf
Leaf covered in hairs	Hairs trap a layer of still, humid air; this reduces diffusion of water vapour from the interior of the leaf
Stomata sunken in pits or grooves in the leaf	Still, humid air collects in the pits; this reduces the diffusion of water vapour through the stomata

Table 13 Some adaptations of xerophytic leaves

Translocation: source to sink

Plants make a great variety of organic compounds, e.g. they make sucrose for the transport of energy. Leaves make sucrose from the sugars they produce in photosynthesis. Sucrose travels from the mesophyll cells, where it is made, to the companion cells, which pump it across their membranes, and then it passes into sieve tube elements through plasmodesmata. Accumulation of sucrose lowers the water potential inside the sieve tube elements so that water flows in from surrounding cells by osmosis. Hydrostatic pressure builds up inside the phloem sieve tubes, which forces the sugary solution from cell to cell through the sieve tubes and away from the leaves. Phloem sap flows from the leaves to meristems (growth areas), roots, new leaves, flowers, fruits and seeds. At these 'sinks', sucrose and other assimilates are removed from the sieve tubes, which lowers the hydrostatic pressure. This maintains a pressure gradient from source to sink. Phloem sap may move in opposite directions in adjacent sieve tubes, unlike the flow of water in xylem, which is always one-way — upwards from roots to leaves. Mass flow in phloem is maintained by an active mechanism. There are several lines of evidence for this:

- The rate of flow is higher than can be accounted for by diffusion.
- Companion cells and sieve tube elements have mitochondria and use ATP to drive pumps to move sucrose. They achieve this by pumping H^+ out of the cell. H^+ diffuses back into the cell through a carrier protein, which also transports sucrose.

Some scientists have questioned this mechanism, because some protein fibres within sieve tubes have no function in the mass flow process.

Links In the qualitative question for Unit F213, you may be asked to look at microscope slides showing sections of root, stem or leaf and then to draw low-power plan diagrams and detailed high-power drawings. You may be asked to compare the leaf of a plant such as marram grass, which has adaptations for reducing water loss, with a leaf without these adaptations.

It is a good idea to revise the details about osmosis and water potential in Module 1 (see pp. 25–26) for this section on transport in plants. You are expected to apply your understanding of these topics to the absorption of water from the soil by root hairs and the transfer of water through a plant. If asked about water, always use the terms 'osmosis' and 'water potential', and explain that water moves '*down* a water potential gradient'. The membranes of root hair cells contain aquaporins for absorption of water by osmosis and carrier proteins for the absorption of ions by facilitated diffusion and active transport (see pp. 23–24). The membranes of guard cells have carrier proteins for moving ions into the cytoplasm by active transport. This occurs so that the water potential inside the guard cells decreases, water enters by osmosis and the cells become turgid. The swelling of guard cells causes the stomata to open. Companion cells have carrier proteins for moving sucrose (see above).

Meristematic cells differentiate into sieve tube elements and companion cells and into xylem vessels (see p. 31). You can work out the changes that occur to the cells as they differentiate by rereading pages 64–65 to decide how a cell like the one in Figure 2 on p. 15 changes into a xylem vessel element, a sieve tube element or a companion cell. You also need to be able to explain how the cells in the xylem and phloem are adapted for their transport functions. You may have to label a drawing or diagram of phloem cells and you will need to recognise structures such as plasmodesmata, sieve plate, mitochondria, nuclei, endoplasmic reticulum and cell walls.

Questions
&
Answers

This section is not exactly like the unit test. Each question represents one of the sections of the unit, but in the unit test you can expect questions to cover more than one section of the unit. There are 60 marks in total.

As you read through this section, you will discover that Candidate A gains full marks for all the questions. This is so that you can see what high-grade answers look like. Remember that the minimum for grade A is about 80% of the maximum mark (in this case around 48 marks). Candidate B makes a lot of mistakes — often these are ones that examiners encounter frequently. I will tell you how many marks Candidate B gets for each question. If Candidate B's overall mark is about 40% of the total (around 24 marks), then he/she will have passed at grade E standard. Use these benchmarks when trying the questions yourself.

The examiners will also assess the quality of your written communication in the unit test. They will indicate the questions where this is assessed.

Examiner's comments

Candidates' answers are followed by examiner's comments. These are preceded by the icon ℮ and indicate where credit is due. In the weaker answers they also point out areas for improvement, specific problems and common errors, such as lack of clarity, weak or non-existent development of ideas or concepts, irrelevance, misinterpretation of the question and mistaken meanings of terms.

Question 1

Cell structure

Insulin is a protein hormone secreted by cells in the pancreas. Figure 1 is a diagram that shows the interrelationships between the organelles involved in production and secretion of insulin from a pancreatic cell.

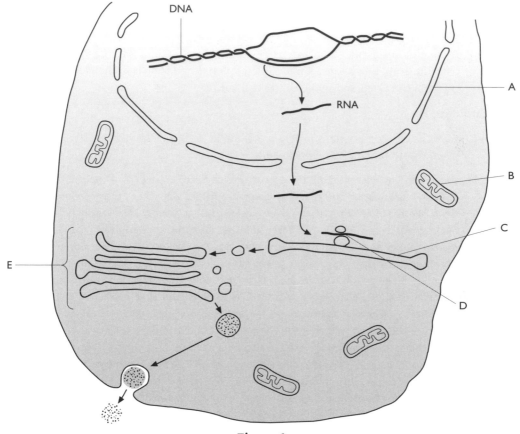

DNA

RNA

A

B

C

D

E

Figure 1

(a) (i) Name the structures A, B and C. (3 marks)

(ii) Describe the functions of structures D and E in the production of protein in the pancreatic cell shown. (4 marks)

(b) Cells make the proteins actin and tubulin, which are not secreted but remain within the cytoplasm to form the cytoskeleton. State three functions of the cytoskeleton. (3 marks)

Total: 10 marks

Candidates' answers to Question 1

Candidate A

(a) (i) **A** = nuclear envelope; **B** = mitochondria; **C** = endoplasmic reticulum

Candidate B

(a) (i) **A** = nucleus; **B** = mitochondrion; **C** = SER

Candidate A

(a) (ii) The ribosome (D) assembles amino acids to make polypeptides. This process is called translation. The polypeptides move through the ER to reach the Golgi apparatus (E), where they are modified and put into vesicles. The vesicles bud off from the Golgi and move to the cell surface.

Candidate B

(a) (ii) D is the ribosome where proteins are made. E is the Golgi apparatus where proteins are modified and packaged.

Candidate A has identified the three structures correctly in part **(i)**. Although label **B** is only pointing to one mitochondrion, examiners will accept *mitochondria* in cases like this. Candidate B has given nucleus rather than nuclear envelope or nuclear membrane. This is not acceptable because the label is pointing to the membranes around the nucleus. Remember that the nuclear envelope is a double membrane structure with a space inside. The endoplasmic reticulum has the same structure. Candidate B has identified **C** as SER (smooth endoplasmic reticulum). Unfortunately, this is incorrect because **C** is *rough* endoplasmic reticulum (RER). Examiners may accept abbreviations, but in a question that asks you to *name* a structure you should write out the name in full. Candidate B gains 1 mark. In part **(ii)**, Candidate A gives two correct statements about *each* structure. Ribosomes assemble amino acids (1 mark) to make polypeptides (1 mark). The answer includes the name of the process, although this is really information that comes in Unit F212 and would not be credited here because it does not answer the question, which says *describe the functions…*, not *state the name of the process…* Candidate A also states that proteins are modified (1 mark) inside the Golgi apparatus and that they are put into vesicles (1 mark). Candidate B has made one correct statement about the ribosome and two about the Golgi apparatus, and gains 3 marks.

Candidate A

(b) The cytoskeleton gives mechanical strength to the cell; transports organelles around inside cells; helps cells like phagocytes move around; moves chromosomes during anaphase of mitosis.

Candidate B

(b) Makes cilia and undulipodia; involved in cell division; moves vacuoles to the cell membrane.

🖉 Three of Candidate A's answers are listed in the specification — you should always know your specification, because this is what you are tested on. Candidate A has given four answers, but the examiner will only mark the first three, so although the fourth one is correct the candidate cannot gain 4 marks. If the first answer was wrong, the examiner would mark the next two and ignore the fourth answer. Candidate B has only given one acceptable answer — the last one. The first one is not a function and the second is too vague.

🖉 Candidate B gains 5 marks out of 10 for Question 1.

Question 2

Cell membranes

(a) Some molecules may cross plasma (cell surface) membranes by simple diffusion. Glucose, however, does not. Explain why glucose cannot cross membranes by simple diffusion. (2 marks)

(b) A student carried out an investigation to find out whether cells take up glucose by facilitated diffusion, by placing animal cells into nine different solutions of glucose. The student determined the rate of uptake of glucose across the plasma (cell surface) membrane into the cells for each solution. The results are shown in Figure 2.

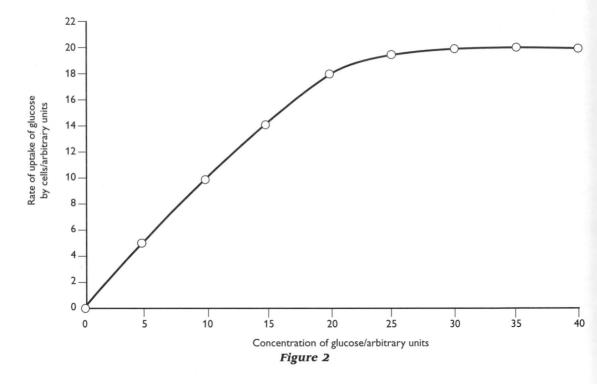

Figure 2

Using the information in Figure 2, explain how the results of the student's investigation support the idea that glucose enters cells by facilitated diffusion. (2 marks)

(c) State one way in which active transport differs from facilitated diffusion. (1 mark)

(d) The student next investigated the movement of water into and out of cells by taking two pieces of epidermis from the scale leaf of a red onion bulb and putting one in distilled water (P) and the other into a concentrated solution of salt (Q). After several minutes, the two pieces of epidermis were mounted on microscope slides using the liquids in which they had been immersed. The student took photographs of cells from each slide (see Figure 3).

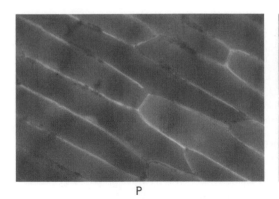 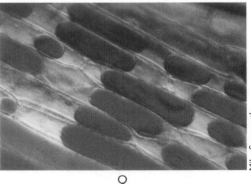

P   Q

Figure 3

Mike Samworth

Explain why the cells in Q have a different appearance compared with those in P. (4 marks)

(e) The student put a drop of some mammalian blood on a microscope slide and added a drop of a concentrated salt solution. The student then looked at the appearance of the red blood cells with the high power of a light microscope.

Describe the appearance of the red blood cells after they had been mixed with a concentrated salt solution. (1 mark)

Total: 10 marks

Candidates' answers to Question 2

Candidate A

(a) Glucose is a large polar molecule, while the membrane consists of a phospholipid bilayer. Phospholipid molecules each have two hydrophobic fatty acid tails. These tails face each other, forming a hydrophobic interior to the membrane that does not permit the passage of (large) hydrophilic molecules like glucose.

Candidate B

(a) Glucose is a large molecule and cannot diffuse across the cell membrane because the gaps between the cell membrane are tiny.

> Candidate B gains a mark for stating that glucose is a large molecule, but the rest of the answer is incorrect. Gaps *between the cell membrane* does not really make sense. The candidate may be thinking about channel proteins as pores that run through the membrane. To gain the second mark there should be something here about the phospholipid bilayer, as given by Candidate A.

Candidate A

(b) For low concentrations of glucose outside the cell, glucose diffuses into the cells, moving down its concentration gradient (as glucose concentration is higher outside the cells than inside them). The rate of uptake increases with concentration. However, after a concentration of about 30 arbitrary units, the rate of

glucose uptake becomes constant because limited numbers of carrier proteins specific to glucose are available. This shows that it is facilitated diffusion, not simple diffusion.

Candidate B

(b) As the concentration of glucose increases, the rate of uptake of glucose also increases but then remains constant and does not decrease or increase.

> The question asks for an *explanation* using evidence from the graph. Candidate B has simply *described* the graph, which gains 1 mark, but there is no explanation, such as that given by Candidate A. If uptake was by simple diffusion you would expect the rate to continue to increase as the concentration of glucose in the external solution increased rather than reaching a plateau at high concentrations of glucose. The carrier proteins have become the limiting factor here — as Candidate A states, there is a limited number of them and there is a limit to the rate at which glucose molecules can move through them. You might think that diffusion of glucose into cells will slow down and stop when the concentration inside the cell is the same as the concentration outside. Cells have a cunning method to maintain the concentration gradient. As soon as glucose molecules enter cells, enzymes convert them into molecules of glucose phosphate. This is a different compound that cannot diffuse out of cells as there is no transport protein for it. This means that the internal concentration of glucose is always very low, so favouring the diffusion of glucose into cells.

Candidate A

(c) In active transport, substances move against a concentration gradient using energy from respiration; in facilitated diffusion, they move down a concentration gradient. This is a passive process because the cell does not use energy to move substances.

Candidate B

(c) Active transport takes place against the concentration gradient using energy from respiration.

> Both answers gain the 1 mark available. Candidate A writes about both active transport *and* facilitated diffusion to make clear the difference. Candidate B gives the two points needed for the mark by writing about active transport *only*. This is acceptable because the question asks how *active transport differs from facilitated diffusion* — Candidate B does just this.

Candidate A

(d) In Q, water has diffused by osmosis out of the cell down its water potential gradient. Most of the water has come from the vacuole and this has decreased in volume, pulling the cytoplasm away from the cell wall. The salt solution fills the space between the cell membrane and the cell wall. P has been in water, so there has been diffusion of water into the cells, making them fully turgid. The cell wall exerts a pressure potential, so the cells reach a maximum size and do not continue to expand.

(e) The cells will have a crinkly appearance.

Candidate B

(d) The cell shows plasmolysis. There is a big space between the cell wall and the cell membrane because water has moved down a concentration gradient.

(e) The cells lose water by osmosis.

> 🖉 Candidate B has not looked at the mark allocation for part **(d)**. There are three ideas in the answer, so even if they were correct they would only gain 3 marks. For a 4-mark question there should be four ideas, if not five or six to be on the safe side. Candidate B has *described* the appearance of the cell rather than *explained* what happened. Notice that Candidate A has used *water potential* in the answer. This is correct — you should never refer to a 'concentration gradient' for water since the movement of water is dependent on a number of factors, not just quantity of water. Sometimes examiners will instruct you to use the term 'water potential' in your answer. The introduction to part **(d)** states that the student was investigating the movement of water. This is a good clue that the question is about osmosis and water potentials. In part **(e)**, Candidate B has given an *explanation* and not a description, which would have been easier to do! Candidate B therefore receives no marks for parts **(d)** and **(e)**.

> 🖉 Candidate B gains 3 marks out of 10 for Question 2.

Cell division, cell diversity and cellular organisation

Stem cells in the bone marrow divide to give rise to cells that become erythrocytes (red blood cells) and neutrophils (a type of white blood cell). Figure 4 shows some stages from the mitotic cell cycle for a stem cell, which gives rise to a mature red blood cell.

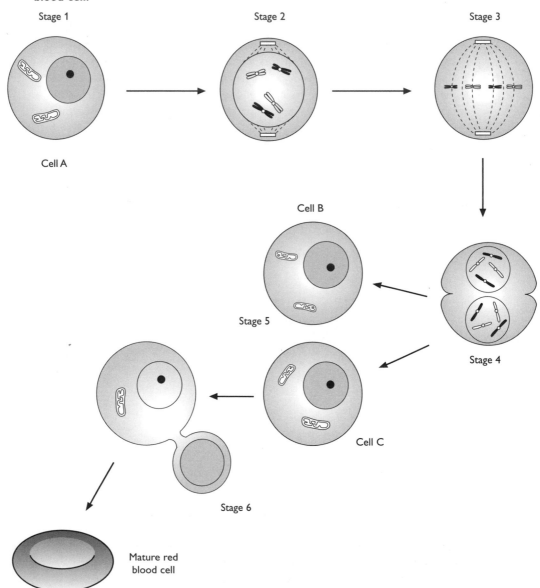

Figure 4

(a) Describe what happens within the nucleus of the stem cell (Cell A) during Stage 1 in Figure 4. (2 marks)

(b) Describe what happens to the chromosomes between Stages 3 and 4. (3 marks)

(c) Outline what happens to Cell C so that it changes into a mature red blood cell. (3 marks)

(d) Explain three ways in which mature red blood cells are adapted for their functions. (3 marks)

(e) State what happens to Cell B after Stage 5. (1 mark)

Total: 12 marks

Candidates' answers to Question 3

Candidate A

(a) DNA is synthesised; the new DNA is checked to make sure that it is an exact copy of the original DNA.

Candidate B

(a) The cell is resting, although it may be making some protein.

> ✍ Candidate B makes a common mistake about interphase by stating that cells are resting. In fact, they are very active (see p. 28). Protein synthesis, as we saw in Question 1, occurs in the cytoplasm, not in the nucleus. It is likely that the cell will be making large quantities of protein during interphase because it has to make new organelles, new membranes and new enzymes. Candidate B gains no marks.

Candidate A

(b) The centromeres of the chromosomes attach to the spindle. The centromeres break so that the two sister chromatids of each chromosome separate from each other. The spindle is made of microtubules which are broken down at the centrioles so the sister chromatids move apart to the poles. The centromeres reach the poles first because they are attached to the microtubules.

Candidate B

(b) When the sister chromatids have reached the poles they de-condense and become thinner. The nuclear envelope reforms and the two new nuclei have the same number of chromosomes as each other and the same number as the nucleus of the parent cell.

> ✍ Candidate B has made the mistake of describing Stage 4, telophase, rather than describing what happens during anaphase, which is the stage between metaphase (Stage 3) and telophase (Stage 4). The examiner could have asked 'what happens during anaphase?', but in this question candidates are being asked to use their knowledge to interpret information from the figure, not simply to recall information. Candidates are often confused by the difference between *chromatid*

and *chromosome*. Strictly speaking, once the centromere has broken the chromatids become chromosomes, because they each contain a complete DNA molecule. Candidate B gains no marks.

Candidate A

(c) Protein synthesis occurs to produce haemoglobin; the organelles such as ER and mitochondria break down; the nucleus is extruded from the cell.

Candidate B

(c) The cell fills up with haemoglobin and loses its nucleus.

> *e* Candidate B has not looked at the mark allocation and has only given two points when at least three are required. The answers from Candidate B are just about the minimum expected, for 2 marks.

Candidate A

(d) They do not have a nucleus, so they contain a large quantity of haemoglobin to carry oxygen. They have a large surface area to volume ratio, so they absorb gases (oxygen and carbon dioxide) easily. Their shape (biconcave disc) gives them a short diffusion distance between the centre of the cell and the membrane.

Candidate B

(d) It has a large surface with much haemoglobin. Red cells have a small surface area to volume ratio. They are small, so they can move through capillaries easily.

> *e* Candidate B has not explained how a large surface is useful. Red blood cells do *not* have a small surface area to volume ratio, they have a large one. The third point about small size would gain a mark. Sometimes these questions refer to the **structure** of the cells, in which case answers about **size** and **shape** are unlikely to gain any marks. Candidate B gains 1 mark here.

Candidate A

(e) Cell B becomes a stem cell and will go through an interphase and divide again.

Candidate B

(e) Cell B remains in the bone marrow.

> *e* Candidate B has identified that cell B remains in the bone marrow, but would not gain a mark because this does not answer the question.

> *e* Candidate B gains 3 marks out of 12 for Question 3.

Exchange surfaces and breathing

A spirometer can be used to measure various aspects of breathing. A 17-year-old athlete was asked to breathe into the spirometer while sitting down. Figure 5 (a) shows the trace that was made. The athlete was then asked to run very fast for a few minutes. Immediately after the athlete stopped exercising, a second trace was taken with the spirometer (shown in Figure 5 (b)). The arrows in both figures indicate when the athlete was breathing through the spirometer.

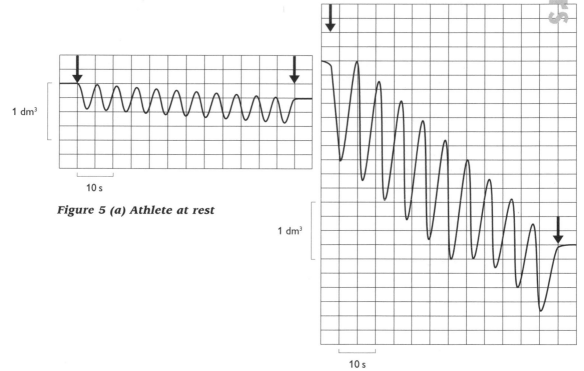

Figure 5 (a) Athlete at rest

Figure 5 (b) Athlete after exercise

(a) Describe how a spirometer is used to measure the oxygen uptake of the athlete.
(4 marks)

(b) Describe how the athlete's breathing after exercise differs from the breathing before exercise, as shown by the traces in Figure 5.

Use the data from the two traces to illustrate the points you make in your answer.

(7 marks)

Total: 11 marks

Candidates' answers to Question 4

Candidate A

(a) The athlete has a nose clip so that he/she breathes in and out through the spirometer and not through the nose as well. When the athlete breathes in, his/her lungs fill with oxygen from the spirometer. Some of this oxygen will be absorbed in the alveoli, so the athlete breathes out less oxygen. He/she breathes out carbon dioxide, but this is absorbed by the soda lime, so it does not go into the spirometer. The athlete does this for a while and the peaks on the spirometer trace decrease gradually. You can measure the rate of uptake of oxygen by measuring the difference in peaks and dividing by the time.

Candidate B

(a) When the athlete breathes in and out you can measure the tidal volume. When he/she takes a deep breath you can measure the vital capacity. The pen attached to the spirometer goes up when the athlete breathes out and goes down when he/she breathes in. That way you can measure the oxygen he/she takes up.

> Candidate B has seen that the trace in Figure 5(a) shows the tidal volume but has not read the question carefully. The trace in Figure 5(a) shows the tidal volume at rest but does not show the vital capacity (see Figure 22 on p. 44). Candidate B gains no marks here. The question asks about *oxygen uptake*, which is determined by measuring the decrease in the peaks over a known period of time, as Candidate A makes clear. In this type of question you may wish to annotate the figure to help show the examiner what you mean. If you do this, make it clear in your answer. For example, you could write 'please see what I have written on Figure 5' so the examiner will look at your annotations.

Candidate A

(b) The athlete takes deeper breaths. The peaks on the graph fall more steeply, which shows the oxygen uptake has increased from 250 cm³ min⁻¹ to 3500 cm³ min⁻¹. Before exercise, the athlete's mean tidal volume (TV) was 0.5 dm³; after exercise it is 2.0 dm³. His/her ventilation rate (TV × breathing rate) was 20 dm³ min⁻¹ after exercise; before exercise it is 5.5 dm³ min⁻¹.

Candidate B

(b) After exercise, the athlete takes deeper breaths, so his/her tidal volume is much larger. He/she breathes slightly more slowly than before exercise as the peaks are further apart. This shows that the athlete's vital capacity is larger after exercise than before, so he/she breathes in a larger amount of air.

> Candidate A has written a concise answer, using data to illustrate the points made. The answer also includes the ventilation rate, which is calculated by multiplying the tidal volume by the breathing rate, to indicate the volume of air moved into the lungs every minute. This is sometimes called the minute volume. Candidate A certainly gains a mark for doing this. Candidate B has not followed the instruction

to use the traces from Figure 5 and has not measured or calculated anything. This means that the marks for use of data cannot be awarded. Candidate B's answer does make two correct observations about tidal volume and rate of breathing, but the third sentence gains no marks. The candidate has noticed that the breathing rate after exercise is slightly slower at 10 breaths per minute rather than 11 breaths per minute, which is what it was before exercise in the trace in Figure 5(a). Figure 5(b) does not show the vital capacity, and in any case vital capacity does not change in so short a time — it only increases after a period of training. The candidate also refers to the *amount* of air, which should be the *volume* of air. Examiners often withhold marks from candidates who use the word 'amount' when they should use terms such as 'volume' or 'concentration'. This is especially important when writing about enzyme practicals (see the Unit Guide for Unit 2). Candidate B gains 2 marks for two correct observations.

Ⓔ Candidate B gains 2 marks out of 11 for Question 4.

Question 5

Transport in animals

(a) Figure 6 shows three stages in the cardiac cycle.

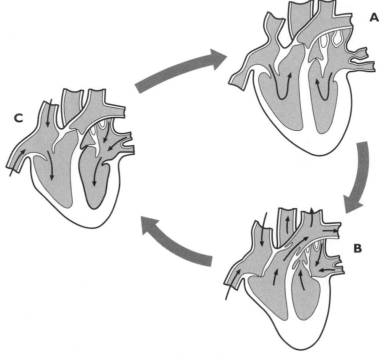

Figure 6

Study Figure 6 carefully and complete the table below to show what is happening to the following parts of the left side of the heart at each of the stages A, B and C:

- left atrium
- left ventricle
- atrioventricular valve
- aortic valve

Stage	Left atrium	Left ventricle	Atrioventricular valve	Aortic valve
A	contracts to force blood into left ventricle	relaxes and fills with blood from left atrium	open	closed
B				
C		relaxes and fills with blood from left atrium		

(5 marks)

(b) Figure 7 shows three electrocardiogram traces. Trace 1 is from a person with a heart showing normal activity. Traces 2 and 3 are from people who have different heart conditions.

ECG trace 1

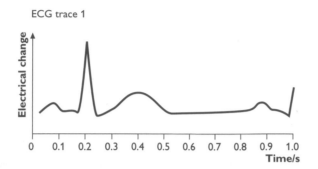

ECG trace 2

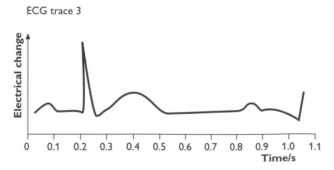

ECG trace 3

Figure 7

Describe the ways in which **ECG** traces 2 and 3 differ from **ECG** trace 1. (4 marks)

Total: 9 marks

Candidates' answers to Question 5

Candidate A

(a)

Stage	Left atrium	Left ventricle	Atrioventricular valve	Aortic valve
A	contracts to force blood into left ventricle	relaxes and fills with blood from left atrium	open	closed
B	relaxes to fill with blood from pulmonary veins	contracts to force blood into aorta (systemic circulation)	closed	open
C	relaxes to fill with blood from pulmonary veins	relaxes and fills with blood from left atrium	open	closed

Candidate B

(a)

Stage	Left atrium	Left ventricle	Atrioventricular valve	Aortic valve
A	contracts to force blood into left ventricle	relaxes and fills with blood from left atrium	open	closed
B	relaxes to fill with deoxygenated blood	contracts to pump blood out of the heart into the aorta	closed	open
C	contracts to pump blood	relaxes and fills with blood from left atrium	open	closed

See Table 7 on p. 49. Candidate B has not noticed that in Stages **B** and **C** it is necessary to say where the blood is going, as in Stage **A**. One mark is awarded for noting the state of the valves in **B** and 1 mark for the state of the valves in **C**. Both candidates get these correct. Re-read pp. 49–51 to make sure you understand what causes the atrioventricular valve and semilunar valve to open and close, because this sometimes causes problems for candidates. Candidate B states that the left atrium fills with deoxygenated blood. This is incorrect. Oxygenated blood flows into the left atrium from the pulmonary veins. Candidate B gains 3 marks.

Candidate A

(b) ECG trace 2 shows no P, Q, R, S and T waves, and there is no regular rhythm. There is very little electrical activity, which means the heart is fibrillating. ECG trace 3 shows a long gap between the *P* wave and the *QRS* wave. This could be due to poor conduction in the Purkyne tissue.

Candidate B

(b) In ECG2 there is no regular pattern, such as the one evident in ECG1, which means the heart is not contracting properly. ECG3 shows a different pattern of electrical activity from ECG1, with a longer gap before the *QRS* wave, of about 0.1 s.

Both candidates make good points about the ECGs. Candidate B refers to ECG1, but it is acceptable to make observations about aspects of ECG2 and ECG3 that are different from ECG1 without specifically mentioning ECG1. Candidate A has given correct explanations, but notice that this was not required by the question. No marks are gained by this extra detail, although it is good to see. Candidate B gains 3 marks — 2 for identifying differences between the ECG traces and 1 for using a figure (0.1s) from ECG trace 3.

Candidate B gains 6 marks out of 9 for Question 5.

Question 6

Transport in plants

Figure 8 shows a transverse section across part of a leaf.

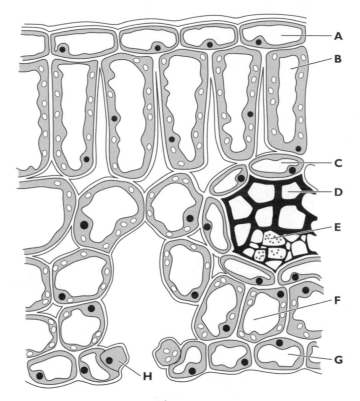

A
B
C
D
E
F
G
H

Figure 8

(a) The letters **A–H** in Figure 8 identify different cells in the leaf. Use the appropriate letters to identify the xylem and phloem. (1 mark)

(b) With reference to Figure 8, explain why transpiration is the consequence of gaseous exchange. (2 marks)

(c) Explain the mechanisms that bring about transport of water in xylem vessels. In your answer, you should use appropriate technical terms, spelled correctly. (5 marks)

Total: 8 marks

Candidates' answers to Question 6

Candidate A

(a) xylem = **D**; phloem = **E**.

Candidate B

(a) xylem = **E**; phloem = **D**.

> ℮ Candidate B has got the answers the wrong way around. This is a very common mistake. In leaves, phloem is below the xylem. Two other clues in Figure 8 are: the walls of the xylem vessels are shown as very thick; some of the phloem sieve tubes have sieve plates, e.g. the cell labelled **E**. No marks for Candidate B.

Candidate A

(b) Inside the leaf there are many air spaces; each cell inside the leaf is in contact with air, making a large surface for absorbing carbon dioxide during the day and absorbing oxygen at night. Water inside the cells diffuses into the cell walls and evaporates from these damp surfaces.

Candidate B

(b) Transpiration is the loss of water by evaporation from the mesophyll inside the leaf and diffusion of water vapour through the stomata. Gases diffuse in and out through the stomata.

> ℮ Candidate A explains that the damp surfaces inside the leaf are the site of gaseous exchange. Candidate B does not do this — it appears that he/she thinks gaseous exchange occurs through the stomata, which is not the case. Gases diffuse through the stomata, but the exchange occurs on the cell walls in much the same way as gaseous exchange occurs in the alveoli (see page 40). These gaseous exchange surfaces have two features in common: they both form a large surface area, and they are thin. Gases circulate within the air spaces inside the plant; there is no equivalent of the blood system found in animals for circulating oxygen and carbon dioxide, so each cell has its own gaseous exchange surface. No marks are awarded to Candidate B.

Candidate A

(c) Water is effectively pulled up xylem vessels due to the evaporation of water from the damp cell walls of the mesophyll cells and the diffusion of water vapour to the atmosphere. The transpiration pull along the length of the vessels depends on two types of force: cohesion, a force of attraction between water molecules, and adhesion, a force of attraction between two unlike molecules, in this case water molecules and the cellulose walls of the vessels. This cohesion-tension allows net movement of water in an unbroken, continuous column known as mass flow.

Candidate B

(c) Root hair cells absorb water by osmosis. Water travels across the cortex of the root through the apoplast and symplast pathways until it reaches the endodermis,

where the Casparian strip prevents water travelling by the apoplast pathway. The endodermal cells in the root actively pump solutes and ions into the bottom of the xylem vessel and make a water potential gradient, causing water to move into the xylem vessels by osmosis.

When explaining how water moves through the xylem, always start your explanation with transpiration in the leaves and refer to **transpiration pull** as Candidate A has done. Candidate A has also included appropriate technical terms, so gains full marks. Candidate B has described movement of water into the root and across the root cortex. This is not transport *in the xylem* so cannot gain any marks. Candidate B gets 0 marks out of 8 for Question 6.

Overall, Candidate B gains 19 marks. This is not enough for an E grade.

You can see that Candidate B has lost marks for a number of different reasons.

- Some answers are not developed fully, e.g. Q.1 (b), Q.6 (b).

- Appropriate terms have not been used, e.g. Q.2 (a), Q.6 (c)

- Structures have not been named in full, e.g .Q.1 (a)(i).

- Command words have not been followed, e.g. Q.2 (b), where the candidate described rather than explained, and Q.2 (e), where there was an explanation rather than a description. See p. 5 for advice about 'Describe' and 'Explain'.

- The mark allocation has not been followed, e.g. Q.2 (d), Q.3 (c).

- Instructions have not been followed carefully, e.g. Q.4 (b).

- Data provided have not been used in answers, e.g. Q.4 (b).

- Answers are not precise enough, e.g. Q.4 (b), where the candidate uses the word 'amount' rather than 'volume'.

- Common errors have been made: Q.3 (a), where the cell was said to be 'resting' during interphase; Q.4 (d), stating that red blood cells have a 'small' surface area-to-volume ratio', when they have a large SA:V ratio; Q.4 (b), stating that vital capacity is larger after exercise, when it isn't; Q.6 (a), confusing the positions of xylem and phloem; Q.6 (b), stating that gaseous exchange in leaves occurs through stomata, when it occurs on all the cell surfaces in the leaf.

- Not answering the question, e.g. Q.2 (e), Q.4 (a).

- In Q.6 it is clear that Candidate B has neglected to learn the plant biology effectively. Plants are important — we would not be here without them!